THE COMPLETE BOOK OF

INDIAN COOKING

THE COMPLETE BOOK OF
INDIAN COOKING

Edited by
Veronica Sperling & Christine McFadden

SMITHMARK

Distributed in the USA by SMITHMARK Publishers,
a division of U.S. Media Holdings Inc.,
16, East 32nd Street, New York, NY 10016

First published in the UK in 1996

SMITHMARK books are available for bulk purchase for sales promotion and premium
use. For details, write or call the manager of special sales, SMITHMARK publishers,
16 East 32nd Street, New York, NY 10016; (212) 532-6600

ISBN: 0-76519-685-9

10 9 8 7 6 5 4 3 2 1

Printed in Italy

Produced by Haldane Mason, London

Acknowledgements
Art Direction: Ron Samuels
Design: Digital Artworks Partnership Ltd

Material contained in this book has previously appeared in
Classic Indian Cooking and *Indian Side Dishes* by Cara Hobday
Quick & Easy Indian Cooking and *Indian Vegetarian Cooking* by Louise Steele
Balti Cooking by Jenny Beresford
Recipes with Yogurt by Pamela Westland

Contents

INDIAN CUISINE

The cuisine of India offers a whole range of mouthwatering recipes to the adventurous cook. Every region of this vast nation has its own favorite ingredients, flavorings, and methods of cooking, and the variety of dishes is extensive. This book contains a complete collection of recipes for all tastes and occasions. Whether you want a quick and easy meal or a complete Indian-style dinner, you'll find everything you need, right down to the appetizers and drinks, to capture the flavor of India.

INDIAN REGIONAL COOKING

With India's vast geographical range and varied natural resources, cooking is highly regional. In the past, difficult transportation meant that cooks could not obtain fresh ingredients from other parts of the country, so local dishes developed, making the most of available produce. The number of religions throughout India also has a strong influence on food and cooking, as each has its own strict dietary code.

The diversity of Indian cuisine is most obvious in the contrast between the rich, meat-based dishes served with bread in the northern states of Punjab, Kashmir, and Uttar Pradesh, and the spicy-hot, pulse-based vegetarian cuisine of the south, where rice is the staple accompaniment.

Northern India

Even today, food from the north reflects the influence of Muslim Moguls who conquered India in the sixteenth century. The invaders brought with them a love of good living and rich Persian recipes for fragrant and flavorful rice dishes, such as the nut and fruit pilaus and the saffron-flavored meat and rice casseroles called biryanis. Mogul courts located in northern cities became the sites of lavish banquets and great feasts; gold and silver platters were piled high with mounds of subtly flavored and beautifully colored foods, garnished with thin leaves of pounded silver called vark. This legacy lives on, in that the food prepared for today's great celebrations – weddings, births, family gatherings – will be Mogul-style dishes.

Other popular dishes that reflect the Mogul influence, both locally and on Indian restaurant menus around the world, include kormas – braised meat in creamy sauces – and koftas – spicy meatballs that are broiled, then slowly cooked in rich sauces. Dishes from these areas often include the words mughlai and shahi in their titles. Mughlai food is spicy and rich, as it is traditionally cooked in ghee. Cream and almonds are regular ingredients in these dishes. The southern city of Hyderabad is an exception to the north/south divide as the richness of northern-style Mogul cooking continues here today.

Punjab is also the home of tandoori dishes, where marinated meat and seafood are cooked in clay ovens called tandoors which are positioned over charcoal or wood-burning fires. Tandoori chicken is probably the best-known tandoori dish, but leavened naan breads are also cooked on the sides of the oven. Modern homes rarely include tandoori ovens, so the broiler or outdoor barbecue are more commonly used. Purists say the results are not the same, but the food is still dry on the outside and tender and succulent inside.

Large numbers of Indians living in the north of the country are Hindus, to whom the cow is sacred, so beef is rare. Fragrant long-grain basmati rice, grown in the foothills of the Himalayas, forms the basis of the pilaus and biryanis.

Southern India

Rice is served with every meal in the southern regions of India, and as it doesn't grow there, it has to be transported from the north. Rice is used to absorb the characteristic liquid-style curries and is served with pulse-based dishes to provide protein – vital in an area which is overwhelmingly vegetarian.

In the hot and humid eastern plains that surround Bengal, the mustard plant flourishes, providing oil for

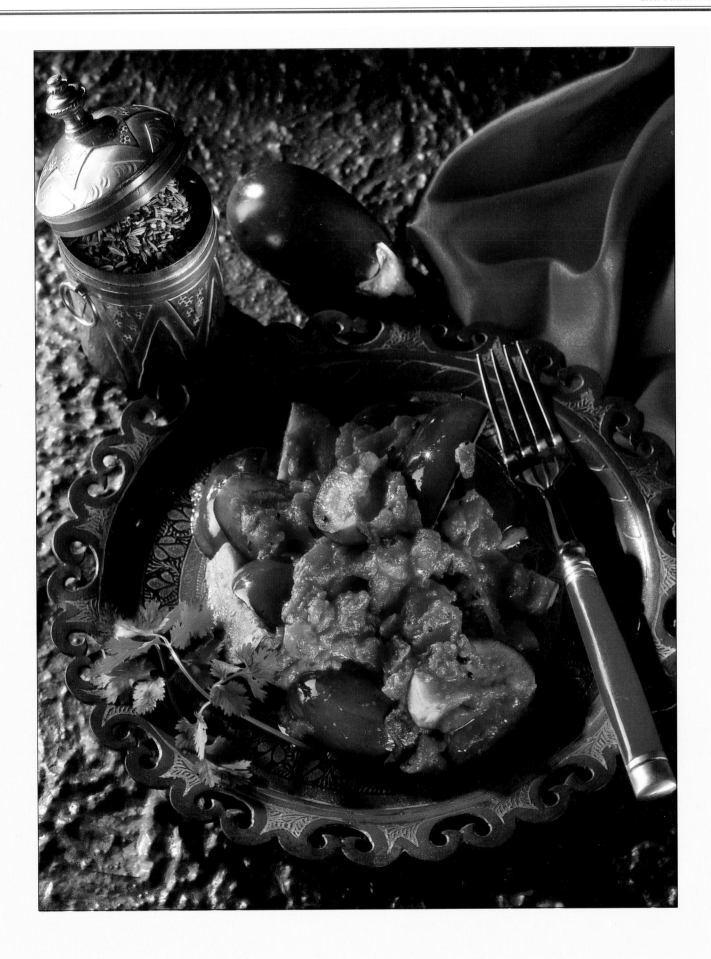

cooking and spicy seeds for flavoring. Rice and seafood appear in many meals, often flavored with mustard oil.

Seafood, coconut, and fresh chilies are cooked in endless combinations in the western coastal regions around Goa. This is the home of the ultra-hot vindaloo curries, given a distinctive hot and sour flavor by local chilies and vinegar. Christian communities were established here when the region was conquered by the Portuguese, and their influence means that pork vindaloos are found, unlike areas with large Muslim or Hindu populations. The region is also the home of 'Bombay Duck'. Neither from Bombay nor a duck, it is a small fish that is dried in the sun and sold in thin strips.

In hot Madras and the surrounding southern states, highly-spiced grains and lentils make up a substantial part of the daily diet, with rice and lentils often combined in a single dish. Meals also include a selection of the lush exotic fruit that thrive in the hot, tropical climate. Bananas are a daily snack, while the trees' large, shiny green leaves are used traditionally as serving platters instead of plates.

INDIAN MEALS

Traditionally, all the dishes in an Indian meal are served at once, without any concept of courses. Although Indian restaurants in the West follow our style of serving different courses, this is not the way in typical Indian homes, whether they are vegetarian or meat-eating families. A meal in a meat-eating home will consist of a meat dish, a vegetable dish, a pulse dish, a chutney or relish for accompaniment and, in the south, a large bowl of steaming rice or, in the north, freshly-baked bread. Each of the dishes is selected to provide a harmonious blend of flavors. The meal may be served in individual bowls for the diners to help themselves, or each person may have their own thali – a large metal plate with individual bowls on it.

Creamy Indian ice–cream (kulfi), a dessert, or fresh fruit may be served as a last course. In the north as well as the south, it is customary for Indians to eat with the fingers of the right hand, rather than cutlery, except possibly when entertaining Western guests. Northern diners use just their fingertips or pieces of flat, unleavened bread, such as chapatis, while southerners are quite skilled at using their whole hand. It is not acceptable to use the left hand while eating as it is considered unclean.

Indians have a sweet tooth and like to eat various candies throughout the day, bought from special stores or on street corners. Many are brightly colored and all are very sweet, flavored with coconut, nuts, or rose water. Such candies are an essential part of many religious celebrations.

INDIAN DRINKS

When serving spicy dishes be sure to have plenty of refreshing drinks to hand – chilled mineral water, iced water, and fruit juice are ideal. For special occasions and for a deliciously refreshing drink to sip during a hot, spicy meal, serve iced water flavored with whole spices, such as cardamom pods, cumin seeds, or cinnamon sticks.

Wine is generally not a very good accompaniment to an Indian meal as the taste is overpowered by the strong flavors of the food. Instead, serve well-chilled beer.

For a really authentic touch, serve Lassi, the deliciously cooling Indian drink of lightly spiced yogurt. Simply mix 2½ cups of natural yogurt with an equal quantity of water and beat until smooth. For a sweet version, stir in 1 tsp rose water, 4 tsp superfine sugar, the crushed seeds from 4 cardamom pods, and sprinkle with chopped pistachio nuts. For a savory version, stir in ¼ tsp salt, 1 tsp sugar, ¼ tsp roasted crushed cumin seeds, and garnish with fresh mint sprigs. Serve in a pitcher or tall glasses with plenty of crushed ice.

INGREDIENTS

It's never been easier to create quick and authentic-tasting Indian food thanks to the marvelous range of exciting spices, herbs, and ready-prepared products so widely available. All the ingredients used in the recipes are easy to find in large supermarkets and Asian grocery stores.

Chilies

Much of the heat in Indian dishes comes from the use of fresh chilies, although dried and ground chilies are also commonplace in Indian kitchens. In southern India, with its searingly hot temperatures, chilies are used in copious amounts because they cause the body to perspire, which has a cooling effect. It's not surprising, therefore, that southern India is home to the fiery vindaloo curries. Numerous varieties of fresh chili grow in India and they come in a range of sizes and intensities, from mild to very hot. As a general rule, the smaller a chili, the hotter it will be.

The heat in a chili comes from a substance in the core and the seeds. Although most recipes specify deseeded chilies, it is really a matter of personal taste. If you do not want your dish to be too hot, cut the chili in half lengthwise and remove the seeds and core with the tip of the knife before you chop the chili. Wear rubber gloves or wash your hands afterwards, otherwise your face, eyes, or mouth will sting if you touch them.

Fresh chilies will keep for about five days in the refrigerator.

Coconut

Fresh coconut milk is unmistakable in both savory and sweet dishes from the area around Goa and in many of the vegetarian dishes of southern India. Coconut milk and the freshly grated flesh are regularly included in rich seafood curries, and the flesh is often added to chutneys for its slightly crunchy texture as well as its flavor.

Before you buy a coconut, give it a good shake to make sure you can hear plenty of liquid sloshing around inside; the more liquid it has, the fresher it will be. Use a hammer and screwdriver or the tip of a sturdy knife to poke out the three soft 'eyes' in the top, and shake out all the coconut water. Use

the hammer to tap the coconut around the center until it splits in half. Crack the coconut halves into manageable pieces, then break away the shell. Peel off the thin brown skin. You can then grate the white coconut flesh by hand or in a food processor. The grated flesh will freeze for up to three months and can be used straight from frozen in curries and other cooked dishes.

Coconut milk and creamed coconut

When fresh coconut isn't available, these two ingredients are ideal for adding an authentic Indian flavor to sweet and savory dishes. Coconut milk is sold in cans or as a powder which needs to be made up with water. Creamed coconut is sold in compressed bars and can be added directly to dishes, or dissolved in water first. It gives a richer flavor and texture than canned or powdered coconut milk. You can make coconut milk by soaking unsweetened shredded coconut in water and then straining it through cheesecloth, and squeezing out all the flavored liquid. Do not confuse creamed coconut with coconut cream, which is a very sweet, thick, syrupy mixture used in cocktails.

Garlic

Native to India, garlic adds its sharp, distinctive flavor to dishes throughout the country, and is one of the essential ingredients of the rich Mogul dishes from northern India. It is also popular for flavoring vegetarian dishes, when it is often teamed with fresh ginger. Garlic keeps well at room temperature providing the room isn't too warm, in which case it should be stored in the refrigerator.

Ghee

Many Indian recipes specify using ghee as the cooking fat. This is because it is similar to clarified butter in that it can be heated to a very high temperature without burning. Ghee adds a nutty flavor to dishes and a glossy shine to sauces. You can buy ghee in cans, and a vegetarian version is also available. Store at room temperature or keep in the refrigerator.

If ghee is not available, you can substitute a mixture of sunflower oil and butter – the oil prevents the butter from burning when heated.

Ginger

Spicy vegetarian and Mogul dishes often contain ginger for its characteristic flavor and aroma. The gnarled pale brown roots are sold in supermarkets and Asian grocery stores. Peel before use, then grate or chop finely. Indian cooks often pound ginger into a paste with onions and other spices, and in Mogul cooking a classic flavoring combination is ginger, garlic, and onions, often pounded together. Although ground ginger is a popular ingredient in Western baking recipes, do not substitute it for fresh ginger in savory Indian recipes.

Gram flour

Also called besan flour, this pale yellow flour is made from ground garbanzo beans. In Indian kitchens it is used to make breads, bhajis, and batters, to thicken sauces, and stabilize yogurt when it is added to hot dishes. Buy it from Asian grocery stores or large health food stores and store in a cool, dark place in an airtight container.

Herbs

Indian cooks use many fresh herbs to balance spicy flavors and to add freshness to dishes. To release their full flavor, fresh herbs should be bruised or chopped just before cooking.

BASIL, CILANTRO, MINT, AND PARSLEY are popular fresh herbs in Indian cooking. Only the leaves of basil and mint are used. However, if you're adding parsley or cilantro to a dish, the finely chopped stalks as well as the leaves may be used as they also contain flavor. Cilantro looks like flat-leaf parsley, but it has a more pronounced flavor and the two herbs are not interchangeable. When you buy fresh herbs, look for firm stalks and leaves which look like they have 'bounce' in them: limp and yellowing leaves are a sign that the herb is not fresh. To store herbs, rinse off any dirt and immerse the stems in water

up to their leaves. They will keep in a cool place for up to four days. Fresh leaves can also be finely chopped and frozen in small containers so they can be used straight from the freezer.

Dried, freeze-dried, and frozen herbs are great stand-bys when fresh ones aren't available. You can extract extra flavor from dried herbs if you warm them in the oven before you use them. Just spread them out on a cookie sheet and place in a preheated low oven for 3–4 minutes until they become fragrant. You will be able to smell the aroma when they are ready.

Nuts

Pale green pistachios, cashews, and almonds are regular ingredients in both savory and sweet Indian cooking. The nuts are used both whole and finely ground, often as a thickener for sauces. Freshly ground nuts have the best flavor as grinding releases their natural oils, so it's best to buy nuts whole and grind them yourself, rather than using packets of ready-ground nuts.

Oils

Indian cooks use a variety of vegetable oils.

GROUNDNUT OR SUNFLOWER OIL are good for most dishes, although more specialty oils are sometimes called for.

COCONUT OIL Particularly popular in southern and western India, this oil is extracted from coconut flesh and has a fairly mild taste.

MUSTARD OIL In Bengal, cooks favor this dark golden oil with a pungent flavor. It is also used in pickles throughout India.

SESAME OIL Unlike Chinese sesame oil, the Indian variety is light and colorless. Spices are often fried in it before being combined with other ingredients.

Pulses (legumes)

Dried beans, peas, and lentils are essential ingredients in Indian cooking which is renowned for its interesting and delicious range of pulse dishes, usually known as dal. Pulses are especially valuable in vegetarian homes where, combined with a grain dish and a dairy product, they provide one of the main sources of protein.

When you buy dried pulses, always check the package for any small stones or husks, and remove them before cooking. Dried pulses keep for up to six months in an airtight container, after which the skins begin to toughen, so buy your pulses from a store with a fast turnover. Do not season pulses until after cooking as the salt may also cause them to become tough. Never overlook the option of using canned pulses, which simply need draining and rinsing before use. As canned beans and peas tend to be quite soft in texture, they are usually added to dishes toward the end of the cooking time to prevent their becoming too soft.

With the exception of lentils, all whole, dry pulses need an overnight soak before cooking. Alternatively, for a quicker method, place the pulses in a pan, cover with water, bring to a boil, and boil for 10 minutes. Remove from the heat, cover, and leave to soak for 3 hours. Drain and place the pulses in a clean pan, cover with fresh water, and bring to a boil. Boil hard for 10 minutes, then simmer for the amount of time specified in the recipe.

This second boiling is important to kill poisonous enzymes present in some pulses. The total cooking time will depend on the freshness of the pulses: the fresher they are, the quicker they will cook.

The following pulses are frequently used in Indian cooking:

BLACK-EYED PEAS These oval-shaped peas are gray or beige with a dark dot in the center. They have a slightly smoky flavor. They are sold canned as well as dried.

CHANNA DAL Similar to yellow split peas in appearance, they are husked and split black garbanzo beans. The grains are smaller and the flavor slightly sweeter than that of yellow split peas which you will also see sold as channa dal.

GARBANZO BEANS Cream colored and resembling a hazelnut in appearance, these beans have a nutty flavor and slightly crunchy texture. Indian cooks grind them to make a flour called gram or besan, which is used to make breads, to thicken sauces, and to make batters for deep-fried dishes, such as onion bhajis.

LENTILS As well as the familiar green-brown variety of lentils, Indians also cook a great deal with the milder flavored split red and yellow lentils. All varieties have the advantage of not needing presoaking or boiling before cooking, which makes them the most convenient pulses to use. Be careful not to overcook lentils or they will be reduced to a pulpy mess.

RED KIDNEY BEANS Popular to use in spicy stews, soups, and sauces, these beans have a nutty flavor and are readily available dried and canned. If using dried beans, don't forget to boil them hard for 10 minutes before simmering. This is essential to kill a poisonous enzyme they contain. Canned red kidney beans, however, do not need boiling.

Rice

Long-grain rice is an important ingredient in Indian cooking, especially for vegetarians and in southern India where bread is rarely served. Basmati rice, grown in the Himalayan foothills, has long, slender grains with a delicate flavor that sets it apart from other long-grain rices and accounts for its higher price. You can substitute American or Patna long-grain rice for basmati, but the result will not be quite so good. Easy-cook and brown versions of basmati rice are sold in supermarkets.

To cook basmati rice, put 1 1/2 cups of rice in a fine strainer and rinse under cold running water until the water runs clear. Put the rice in a bowl, cover with fresh water, and leave to soak for 30 minutes.

Drain the rice and transfer to a heavy-based saucepan. Add enough water to cover the rice by 1 inch. Bring to a boil over a high heat, then stir well. Cover the pan tightly, turn off the heat, and leave for 25 minutes. Do not be tempted to lift the lid before the time is up, otherwise the steam will escape and the rice will not cook properly.

Remove the pan from the hotplate and leave to stand for a further 10 minutes before removing the lid. Fluff the rice with a fork and serve.

Rose water

The diluted essence extracted from rose petals is a popular ingredient in Indian desserts, and an essential flavoring of many Mogul dishes. It adds an exotic quality to drinks and sweetmeats. Only a few drops are needed to flavor a dish. You can buy it in delicatessens, supermarkets, and Asian food stores.

Spices

Spices play an essential part in Indian cooking but don't let the vast array on supermarket shelves put you off. You will need only a few familiar ones to give your cooking an authentic taste. It is best to buy whole spices and grind them as needed because they keep their flavor and aroma much longer than ready-ground spices. You can grind spices with a pestle and mortar or use a spice grinder or small electric food processor kept just for that purpose. Buy your spices in small quantities and store them in a cool, dark place so they stay fresh and retain their aroma. If you do buy ground spices, however, be sure to check that they are not past the sell-by date as the flavor and fragrance will probably have deteriorated.

Indian cooks use several techniques to coax all the flavor from dried spices and give dishes well harmonized flavors that do not taste raw. One method is to dry-fry or roast whole seeds over a gentle heat. As the spices roast, they begin to jump around in the pan, so it is a good idea to use a heavy-based skillet with a lid. Dry-frying takes only a few minutes and you will be able to tell when the spices are ready because of the wonderful fragrance that develops. Be sure to stir the spices constantly and never take your eyes off the pan because the spices can burn very quickly.

DRY-FRIED SPICE MIX Add 1 teaspoon of this handy mixture to rice, pulses, or stews during cooking to give an authentic flavor. Heat a small heavy-based skillet over a medium heat. When it is hot, add 4 tablespoons of coriander seeds and 1 tablespoon of cumin seeds. Fry, stirring constantly, until the seeds turn a few shades darker. You should be able to smell the aroma. Immediately pour the seeds onto a plate and leave to cool. Using a pestle and mortar or a small electric spice grinder, grind the seeds as finely as possible. The mixture will keep in an airtight container for up to one month.

Another technique is to slowly fry the spices in the ghee or vegetable oil that will be used for cooking the other ingredients. This has the advantage of not only bringing out the flavors of the various spices, but also adding spiciness to the cooking oil.

The following are the most common spices used in Indian dishes:

AJOWAN Related to caraway and cumin, these small brown seeds are valued for their digestive properties. They are used in vegetable dishes, especially in southern India, and in breads.

ANISEED Similar to fennel seeds, these small seeds are a popular ingredient in food from the Bengali and Kashmiri regions. They taste and smell similar to licorice. They are also available ground from Indian food stores.

CARDAMOM These small pods contain numerous tiny black seeds which have a warm flavor and are highly aromatic. Green cardamoms are considered the best because of their fine, delicate flavor. Black pods make an adequate substitute, but they have a much stronger flavor. Green cardamoms are also prized for their digestive properties, and some Indians chew them raw after they have eaten extra-spicy curries, to aid digestion and sweeten the breath. Used in both sweet and savory dishes, cardamom pods are usually lightly crushed prior to use to allow the full flavor of the seeds to be appreciated. Whole or crushed cardamom pods are not meant to be eaten, so they should be removed before serving or left on the side of the plate. Some recipes specify using just the seeds rather than the whole pod. To remove the seeds, use the end of a rolling pin or a pestle and mortar to break open the pod and take out the seeds. Ground cardamom is the finely ground pods.

CASSIA This spice comes from the bark of the cassia tree. It is similar in both appearance and flavor to cinnamon but is not quite so uniform in shape. If it is not available, cinnamon can be used in its place.

CAYENNE PEPPER Orange-red in color, this ground pepper is extremely hot and pungent, being made from dried red chilies.

CHILI The quickest way to add heat to a curry or other Indian dish is to add a crumbled dried red chili, or dried chili flakes. For extra heat add the seeds as well.

CINNAMON SHAVINGS of bark from the cinnamon tree are processed and curled to form the sticks of this fragrant spice. The sticks are not edible, although they make an attractive garnish as well as adding flavor to sweet and savory dishes. Cinnamon is also available ground.

CLOVES These dried, unopened flower buds are used to give flavor and aroma to both sweet and savory dishes, but should be used with caution because the flavor can be overwhelming if too many are used. Whole cloves are not meant to be eaten. Cloves are one of the spices traditionally included in garam masala.

CORIANDER Available ground or as seeds, this spice is one of the essential ingredients in Indian cooking. Coriander seeds are often dry roasted before use to develop their flavor.

CUMIN These caraway-like seeds are popular with Indian cooks because of their warm, pungent flavor and aroma. The seeds are sold whole or ground, and are usually included as one of the flavorings in garam masala.

FENUGREEK The seed of this herb is used for its bitter flavor and pronounced aroma, especially in vegetarian dishes and pickles. You will find the seeds and a ground version in Indian grocery stores.

GARAM MASALA This is actually a mixture of ground spices, not an individual spice. The usual combination includes cardamom, cinnamon, cloves, cumin, nutmeg, and black peppercorns, but most Indian cooks have a personal recipe, often handed down for generations. Garam masala is usually added to savory dishes at the end of cooking so the heat doesn't destroy the subtle flavoring. You can buy prepared garam masala at large supermarkets or Asian grocery stores, or you can make your own: finely grind together 2 tbsp cumin seeds, 2 tbsp coriander seeds, 1 tbsp black peppercorns, 2 tsp cloves, 1 tsp cardamom seeds, 2 dried bay leaves, 1 cinnamon stick (about 3 inches), 1 dried red chili. Store in an airtight container and use within three weeks.

MUSTARD SEEDS These tiny, reddish-brown seeds are used throughout India, and are a particularly important ingredient in pickles and in southern vegetarian cooking. The leaves and oil are also included in many dishes. Mustard seeds are often fried in oil or ghee to bring out their flavor before being combined with other ingredients. You can substitute the black seeds more commonly found in Western supermarkets.

ONION SEEDS Always used whole in Indian cooking, these tiny black seeds are added to pickles and often sprinkled over the top of naan breads. Onion seeds don't have anything to do with the vegetable, but they look similar to the plant's seed, hence the name.

PAPRIKA Used for color and flavor, this bright red-orange spice comes from a variety of red pepper. Although similar in color to chili powder and cayenne, paprika has a mild flavor and is used in far greater quantities.

PEPPERCORNS These are available in three colors - white (ripe berries), black (unripened berries dried until dark greenish-black in color), and green (unripe berries). The black berries with their warm, aromatic flavor are most frequently used in Indian cooking. Peppercorns are used whole in dishes such as biryani (they are not meant to be eaten and should be left on the side of the plate), or they may be ground, in which case they should be freshly milled as required as they quickly lose their flavor.

POPPY SEEDS In India, poppy seeds are white, not black, and used for their thickening properties. Look for white seeds in Asian grocery stores and some health food stores; do not substitute black poppy seeds as the flavor is different.

SAFFRON The most expensive of all spices, saffron strands are the stamens of a type of crocus. They give dishes a rich, golden color, as well as adding a distinctive, slightly bitter taste. Saffron is sold as a powder or in strands. Saffron strands are more expensive but do have a superior flavor.

TAMARIND Vegetable dishes are often given a sharp, sour flavor with the inclusion of tamarind juice. This is made from the semi-dried, compressed pulp of the tamarind tree. You can buy bars of the pungent-smelling pulp in Asian grocery stores. Store it in a tightly sealed plastic bag or airtight container.

TURMERIC This aromatic root is dried and ground to produce a distinctive bright yellow-orange powder. It has a warm, aromatic smell and a full, somewhat musty taste.

VARK This is edible silver that is used to decorate elaborate dishes prepared for the most special occasions and celebrations, such as weddings. It is pure silver that has been beaten until it is wafer thin. It comes with a piece of backing paper which is peeled off as the vark is laid on the cooked food. It is extremely delicate and so must be handled with care. You can buy vark in Indian food stores, and remember that because it is pure silver it should be stored in an airtight bag or box so it doesn't tarnish.

Yogurt

Rich in protein and calcium, yogurt plays an important part in Indian vegetarian cooking, as well as in meat dishes. It is used as a marinade, as a creamy flavoring in curries and sauces, and as a cooling accompaniment to hot dishes. Thick natural yogurt most closely resembles the yogurt made in many Indian homes.

When cooking with yogurt, take care not to let it overheat and curdle. To prevent this, stir in the yogurt a spoonful at a time at the end of cooking, making sure each spoonful is fully incorporated before adding the next. Alternatively, you can blend the yogurt with a little cornstarch or gram flour (½ tsp for every ⅔ cup) before adding it to the dish.

COOKING EQUIPMENT

Although Indian cooks are masters of delicious, exotic food, their kitchens are not very differently equipped from those found in Western homes. You won't have to make any major investments in specialty equipment to create authentic-tasting meals.

A large, deep skillet similar to a wok and several heavy-based saucepans or flameproof casseroles are the most important pieces of equipment, as most Indian cooking is done on top of the stove. In fact, Indians don't use anything that is the equivalent of a Western stove. The traditional Indian oven, called a tandoor, was made of clay and built into the ground, but it is more a feature of restaurant cooking today and very few homes have one. In rural areas, cooking is done on a basic coal- or wood-burning stove built near the floor in the corner of the kitchen. The cook squats in front of the stove or sits on a low stool next to it. Here is a guide to the everyday pieces of equipment needed to produce authentic Indian meals.

Blender

Use a blender to quickly mix cooling drinks, such as the yogurt-based lassi. As an alternative, put all the ingredients in a bowl and whip by hand to blend them.

Degchi

This handleless pan is made of aluminum or brass, has a tight-fitting lid, and is similar to the traditional French daubière. Used for cooking slowly-braised dishes, its lid is designed to hold hot coals so ingredients are gently cooked by heat from the top as well as the bottom. A heavy-based flameproof casserole will produce very similar results.

Food processor

Although not essential, modern Indian cooks find a food processor the most efficient way of coping with all the chopping involved in Indian cooking. It is also useful for chopping large amounts of fresh herbs and making pastes from garlic, ginger, and onions. A small food processor or a coffee grinder is ideal for grinding spices. If you choose this option instead of a pestle and mortar, however, remember to use it exclusively for grinding spices as it will flavor any other foods.

Skillet

A non-stick skillet is useful for dry-frying seeds and spices to bring out their flavors before they are ground.

Karahi

This is an Indian version of the versatile Chinese wok. It is used for deep-frying or for slowly simmering meat, poultry, seafood, and pulse dishes. Many Indian homes have two karahis, a deep one with a narrow top which is used for deep-frying, and a shallower one with a much wider top which is used for occasional stir-frying and simmering. Like a wok, it is the curved sides that make this such a useful piece of equipment, because the sides provide a much larger cooking surface than a conventional skillet or saucepan. A traditional Chinese wok is a suitable substitute. Woks come in numerous sizes and are made of various materials, such as cast iron, aluminum, stainless-steel, and even brass. You can also buy woks with non-stick finishes, which are particularly useful if you want to reduce the amount of fat in some recipes. When you buy a wok, look for one with one long wooden handle or two wooden handles on the sides so you can grip it without burning your hands. Some woks, especially those made of cast iron, are very heavy, so it is a good idea to pick one up to make sure you can handle it easily. Most woks need a ring that sits over the burner to keep the wok steady while you cook.

Knives

Indian cooking can involve a great deal of chopping, so firm knives with sharp blades are invaluable. A medium-sized all-purpose knife, called a cook's or kitchen knife, is ideal for most chores, but a flexible, thin-bladed filleting knife is best for filleting fish, and a rigid boning knife is needed for removing meat and poultry bones. Carbon steel can be sharpened very finely, but stainless steel is the usual choice for kitchen knives because it is so easy to take care of. Unlike carbon steel, it doesn't have to be kept dry to prevent it from rusting.

Pestle and mortar

It is easy to buy ground spices and prepared spice mixtures in supermarkets but the flavor of freshly ground spices is vastly superior. A heavy pestle and mortar is useful if you want to grind your own spices. A good quality set will have a slightly rough surface on the interior of the mortar and on the end of the pestle. They may be made from vitrified porcelain, unglazed porcelain, stone, wood, marble, or sometimes even heavy-duty glass.

Saucepans

Several medium saucepans with heavy bases are useful for cooking pulses, rice, and vegetable dishes. The heavy base is important because it helps to distribute heat evenly, and also retains heat once the pan is taken off the heat. Pans with tight-fitting lids mean they can double as casseroles for cooking on top of the stove, which is useful when

you are cooking some of the rice recipes, such pilaus and biryanis. Various materials are used in the manufacture of saucepans and it is a matter of personal choice which you use. Stainless steel is popular because it is hard wearing and easy to clean, but on its own it is not a good conductor of heat. If you want a stainless steel pan, buy one made of heavy-gauge stainless steel or one with copper or aluminum in the base.

Skewers

A supply of stainless steel or bamboo skewers is useful for barbecuing spicy kebabs and some tandoori recipes. Bamboo skewers should be soaked in water for about 30 minutes before use, to prevent their burning. When you buy stainless steel skewers, choose flat, rather than round ones as these hold the ingredients in place when you turn the skewer. If you rub the skewer with vegetable oil before you put any food on it, the cooked food will come off easily.

Tava

This is the traditional flat griddle used for cooking some Indian breads. A large skillet makes an adequate substitute.

Thali

A large rimmed metal plate that comes with several metal bowls, called katoris. Use thalis if you want to serve your Indian meal in the authentic way. Each person has their own thali, with a portion of each dish in each bowl. Made of aluminum or brass (sometimes silver or even gold), thalis are available from Asian grocery stores.

Tongs

A pair of long-handled tongs are essential for lifting sizzling food from hot fat when you are deep-frying, or for turning ingredients under a hot broiler.

COOKING TECHNIQUES

The names of Indian cooking techniques are often incorporated into recipe titles on menus. Some of the ones you are most likely to encounter are included in the following list.

Barbecuing

Before modern kitchens were installed, much of the cooking in India was done over coal or wood fires, and barbecued food remains a favorite. Tandoori chicken, marinated in yogurt and spices which give its glorious reddish-brown color, is a popular dish for barbecuing, as are all forms of kebabs.

Bhaghar

This is a simple technique which adds richness and flavor to meat, fish, vegetable, and especially pulse dishes, and counteracts bland flavors. Ghee or vegetable oil is heated in a heavy-based skillet, then whole spices and seeds are added, and fried until they are golden brown and sizzling. The contents of the pan are poured over the dish a few minutes before serving. The dish is kept covered until ready to serve, to retain all the aromas.

Bharta

This term describes puréed vegetables. Eggplant are often prepared in this way, first being cooked over a charcoal or wood fire so they develop a smoky flavor.

Bhoona

Also known as brown frying, this technique involves stir-frying onions, garlic, ginger, and spices until they turn golden brown. Meat and poultry dishes with reddish-brown sauces often begin with this process and it is an important technique in preparing the classic Mogul dishes of northern India. When chopped or sliced onions are prepared this way they are slowly cooked in ghee, or a vegetable oil, until they turn golden, then the spices are stirred in, and the stir-frying continues until the onions lose all their moisture and turn a dark, rich brown.

Sukka bhoona in a title indicates that the dish has been sautéed, and this style of dish is usually made with the best and tenderest cuts of meat.

Curry

The word 'curry' has become a universal term for Indian cooking and food. Although a dish called a curry does exist, this single word does not do justice to the richly varied dishes and cooking styles of the Indian sub-continent. It is simply a Western way of pronouncing 'kari', a southern Tamil word for sauce or the fragrant leaves of the kari tree. These dried leaves are a main ingredient in a spice mixture called kari podi, which has become known as curry powder. Authentic curries are cooked slowly and never include a marinade, yogurt, or cream as in other spicy dishes. Because the cooking process is so slow and gentle, meat curries are usually made with meat from older animals or the tougher cuts. When vegetables such as peas or potatoes are included in a meat curry, they are usually added toward the end of the cooking time.

Do pyaza

A slowly-braised dish combining both cooked and raw onions. The main ingredient, usually meat, is gently cooked with half the onions until very tender, then a second batch of raw onions is stirred in toward the end of cooking to give extra texture and taste. Traditional recipes use 2 lb onions for each 1 lb meat. You will also see this dish spelled as dopiaza.

Dum

Similar to pot-roasting, this is the Indian method of cooking ingredients in a tightly-sealed container on top of the stove. Traditionally, a pan called a degchi is used, set over hot ashes and with hot coals in its lid. A flameproof casserole is a good substitute, as long as it can be tightly sealed. One method of sealing a container is to make a simple flour and water dough, form it into a roll, place it around the rim, and press down the lid. Alternatively, put a large piece of foil under the lid and scrunch the over-hanging foil around the sides.

Korma

These are slowly-braised dishes, many of which are the rich and spicy, Persian-inspired Mogul dishes served on special occasions. Yogurt is often featured, both as a marinade and as the cooking liquid. In a properly cooked korma, prime tender cuts of meat are used, and the small amount of cooking liquid is absorbed by the meat to produce a deliciously succulent result. A heavy-based cooking container with a tight-fitting lid is essential for a korma.

Marinating

This is a technique widely used to add flavor and tenderize less expensive cuts of meat and seafood before they are baked or broiled, or cooked in a traditional tandoor oven. Sometimes the ingredients are cut into small pieces and submerged in a marinade, while in other recipes the marinade is brushed onto whole fish or chicken breasts. Heavily-spiced yogurt is a popular marinade, especially for ingredients that are cooked over charcoal, under a broiler, or in a tandoor. The yogurt turns into a thin crust as it cooks, protecting the flesh beneath. Lemon and lime juices are also used for marinating, as well as papaya, which has a tenderizing effect.

Talawa

This refers to meat, seafood, poultry, or vegetables that are coated in crumbs or a batter and deep-fried until golden on the outside and tender in the center. You will also see these dishes referred to as talana.

APPETIZERS

Whether you are planning a full-scale dinner party, an informal buffet, or a nourishing family meal, don't forget to include a starter or a few appetizers to tease the tastebuds at the beginning of the meal. Starters or hors d'oeuvres are not generally served as such on an Indian menu – all the dishes are served at once, rather than as separate courses. However, as some people may prefer to eat Indian food in a Western way, dishes such as chicken koftas, butterfly shrimp, or spicy mini kebabs make for a typical beginning. Use hot spices cautiously in such palate-enticing dishes, and serve with a yogurt and cucumber cool dipping sauce. Alternatively, do as the Indians do and serve a selection of snack foods, such as bhajis and pakoras, before the main meal. These make perfect finger food to serve with drinks.

Many of these dishes would also be ideal for taking on a picnic – a favorite Indian family pastime. A common Sunday activity is to take a picnic to the town maidan or green space, and spend a long lazy afternoon with family and friends chatting, eating, and snoozing, and maybe pitching a few cricket balls at a makeshift wicket!

Butterfly Shrimp

These shrimp look stunning when presented on the skewers,
and they will certainly be an impressive prelude to the main meal.

SERVES 2-4

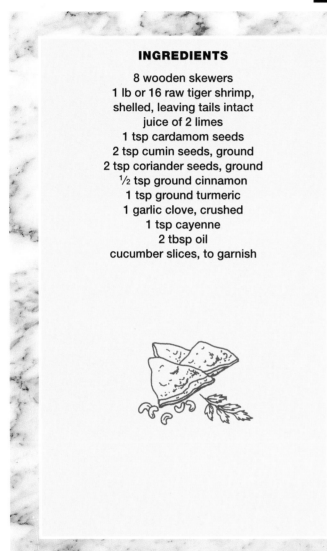

INGREDIENTS

8 wooden skewers
1 lb or 16 raw tiger shrimp,
shelled, leaving tails intact
juice of 2 limes
1 tsp cardamom seeds
2 tsp cumin seeds, ground
2 tsp coriander seeds, ground
½ tsp ground cinnamon
1 tsp ground turmeric
1 garlic clove, crushed
1 tsp cayenne
2 tbsp oil
cucumber slices, to garnish

1 Soak 8 wooden skewers in water for 20 minutes. Cut the shrimp lengthwise in half down to the tail, so that they flatten out to a symmetrical shape.

2 Thread a shrimp onto 2 wooden skewers, with the tail between them, so that, when laid flat, the skewers hold the shrimp in shape. Thread another 3 shrimp onto these 2 skewers in the same way. Repeat until you have 4 sets of 4 shrimp each.

3 Lay the skewered shrimp in a non-porous, non-metallic dish, and sprinkle over the lime juice.

4 Combine the spices and the oil, and coat the shrimp well in the mixture.

5 Cover and chill for 4 hours.

6 Cook over a hot barbecue or in a broiler pan lined with foil under a preheated broiler for 6 minutes, turning once.

7 Serve immediately, garnished with cucumber and accompanied by a sweet chutney – walnut chutney is ideal.

Step *1*

Step *2*

Step *3*

Minted Onion Bhajis

Gram flour (also known as besan flour) is a fine yellow flour made from garbanzo beans and is available from supermarkets and Asian food shops.

MAKES 12

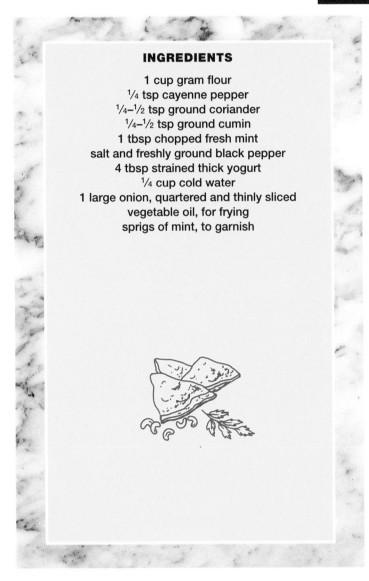

INGREDIENTS

1 cup gram flour
¼ tsp cayenne pepper
¼–½ tsp ground coriander
¼–½ tsp ground cumin
1 tbsp chopped fresh mint
salt and freshly ground black pepper
4 tbsp strained thick yogurt
¼ cup cold water
1 large onion, quartered and thinly sliced
vegetable oil, for frying
sprigs of mint, to garnish

1 Put the gram flour into a bowl, add the cayenne pepper, coriander, cumin, and mint, and season with salt and pepper to taste. Stir in the yogurt, water, and sliced onion and mix well together.

2 One-third fill a large, deep skillet with oil and heat until very hot. Drop heaped spoonfuls of the mixture, a few at a time, into the hot oil and use two forks to neaten the mixture into rough ball-shapes.

3 Fry the bhajis until rich golden brown and cooked through, turning frequently. Drain on absorbent paper towels and keep warm while cooking the remainder in the same way. Serve hot or warm.

Step *1*

Step *2*

Step *3*

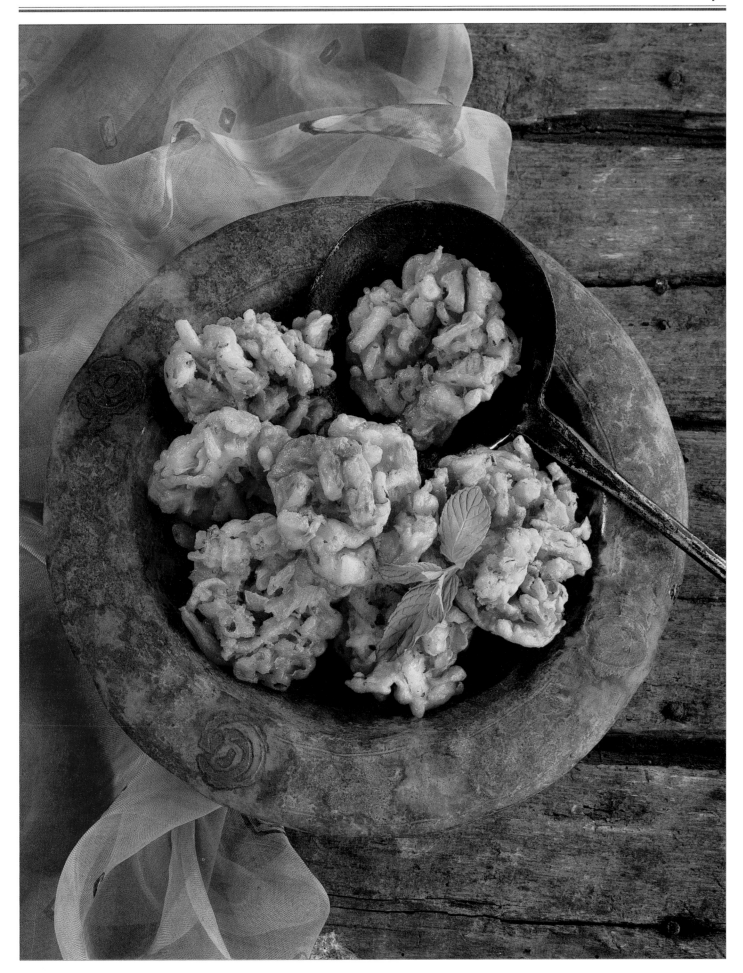

Bite-Size Bajees

Don't be surprised at the shape these form – they are odd but look lovely
when arranged on a tray with the yogurt dipping sauce.

MAKES 20

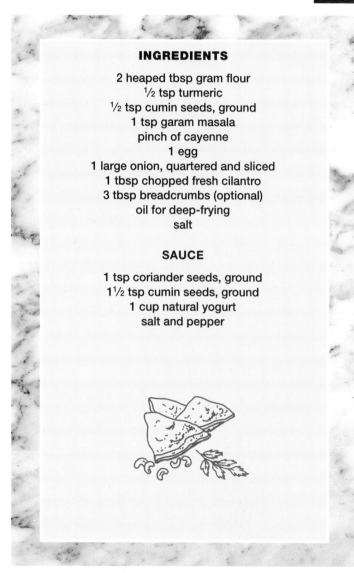

INGREDIENTS

2 heaped tbsp gram flour
½ tsp turmeric
½ tsp cumin seeds, ground
1 tsp garam masala
pinch of cayenne
1 egg
1 large onion, quartered and sliced
1 tbsp chopped fresh cilantro
3 tbsp breadcrumbs (optional)
oil for deep-frying
salt

SAUCE

1 tsp coriander seeds, ground
1½ tsp cumin seeds, ground
1 cup natural yogurt
salt and pepper

1 Put the gram flour into a large bowl and mix in the spices. Make a well in the center and add the egg. Stir to form a gluey mixture. Add the onion and sprinkle on a little salt. Add the cilantro and stir. If the mixture is not stiff enough, add the breadcrumbs.

2 Heat the oil for deep-frying over a medium heat until fairly hot – it should just be starting to smoke.

3 Push a teaspoonful of the mixture into the oil with a second teaspoon to form fairly round balls. The bajees should firm up quite quickly. Cook in batches of 8–10. Keep stirring them so that they brown evenly. Drain on plenty of paper towels and keep them warm in the oven until ready to serve.

4 To make the sauce, roast the spices in a skillet. Remove from the heat and stir in the yogurt. Season well.

Step *1*

Step *3*

Step *4*

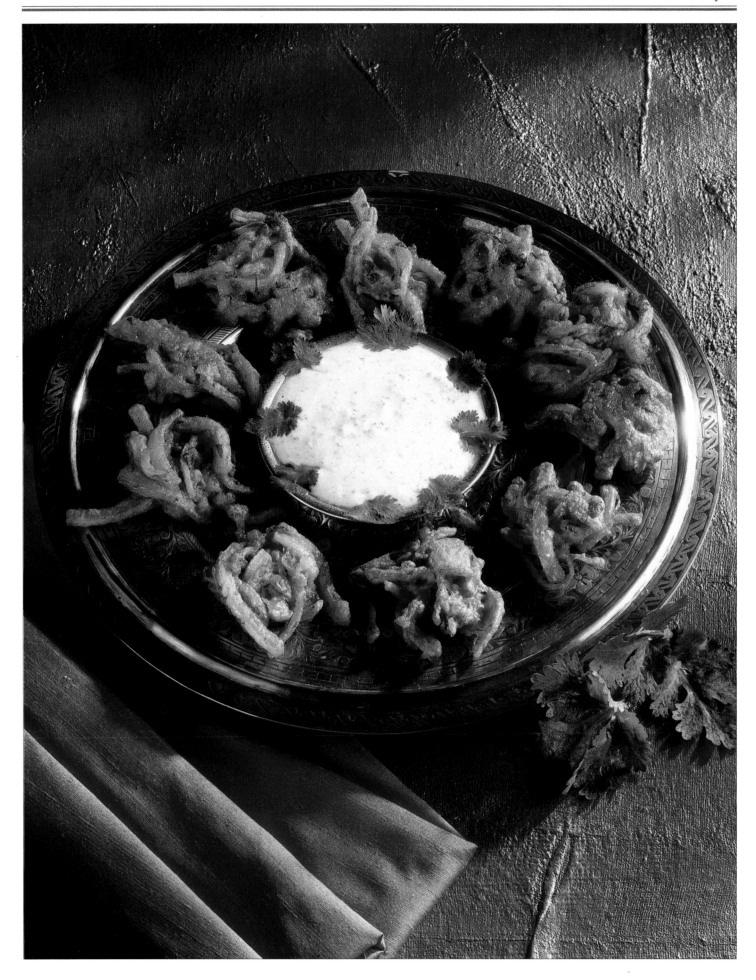

Spicy Bites

*Here are three delicious morsels to whet your appetite before a meal. Use
zucchini with the flowers still attached, if you can find them.*

SERVES 4

INGREDIENTS

SPICED NUTS

1 cup mixed nuts, such as peanuts, cashews, and
blanched almonds
1 dried red chili
1 tsp sunflower oil
1 garlic clove
½ tsp salt
1 tsp garam masala
½ tsp clear honey

MUSSEL MORSELS

2 lb small mussels, scrubbed
3 tbsp mayonnaise
1 tsp garam masala
½ red chili, deseeded and chopped finely
2 scallions, chopped finely
¾ cup white breadcrumbs
salt

DEEP-FRIED ZUCCHINI

1 cup all-purpose flour
½ tsp each turmeric and cayenne
⅔ cup water
2 eggs
vegetable oil
1 zucchini, cut into batons

SPICED NUTS

1 Cook the nuts in a dry, heavy-based pan over a moderate heat until the oil comes off, about 5 minutes. Add the remaining ingredients, except the honey, and cook for a further 3 minutes, stirring frequently. Add the honey and cook for 2 minutes.

2 Remove from the heat and turn into a serving dish.

MUSSEL MORSELS

1 Put a little water in the bottom of a large pan. Discard any mussels that are not firmly closed. Add the mussels and cover the pan. Set over a high heat and leave for 5 minutes; do not uncover. Drain the mussels and discard any unopened ones. Remove the shells and reserve them.

2 Chop the mussel meat finely. Stir the mayonnaise into the mussel meat. Add the remaining ingredients and season to taste. Spoon the mixture back into the shells, and arrange on a plate.

DEEP-FRIED ZUCCHINI

1 Sift the flour and spices together, Add the water, eggs, and 1 tablespoon oil. Beat until smooth.

2 Heat some oil in a wok. Dip the batons into the batter, and drop into the oil. When evenly cooked, remove, and drain on paper towels.

Step *1 : Spiced nuts*

Step *1 : Mussel morsels*

Step *2 : Mussel morsels*

Garlicky Mushroom Pakoras

Whole button mushrooms are dipped in a spiced garlicky batter and deep-fried until golden.

SERVES 6

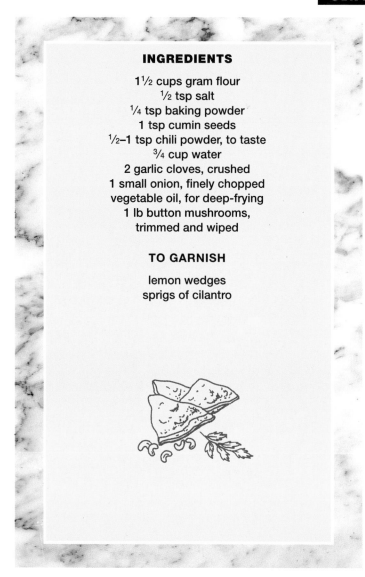

INGREDIENTS

1½ cups gram flour
½ tsp salt
¼ tsp baking powder
1 tsp cumin seeds
½–1 tsp chili powder, to taste
¾ cup water
2 garlic cloves, crushed
1 small onion, finely chopped
vegetable oil, for deep-frying
1 lb button mushrooms, trimmed and wiped

TO GARNISH

lemon wedges
sprigs of cilantro

1 Put the gram flour, salt, baking powder, cumin, and chili powder into a bowl and mix well together. Make a well in the center of the mixture and gradually stir in the water, mixing to form a batter.

2 Stir the crushed garlic and the chopped onion into the batter and leave the mixture to infuse for 10 minutes. One-third fill a deep-fat fryer or pan with vegetable oil and heat to 350°F or until hot enough to brown a cube of day-old bread in 30 seconds. Lower the basket into the hot oil.

3 Meanwhile, mix the mushrooms into the batter, stirring to coat. Remove a few at a time and place them into the hot oil. Fry for about 2 minutes or until golden brown.

4 Remove from the pan with a slotted spoon and drain on paper towels, while cooking the remainder in the same way. Serve hot, sprinkled with coarse salt and garnished with lemon wedges and sprigs of cilantro.

Step *1*

Step *3*

Step *4*

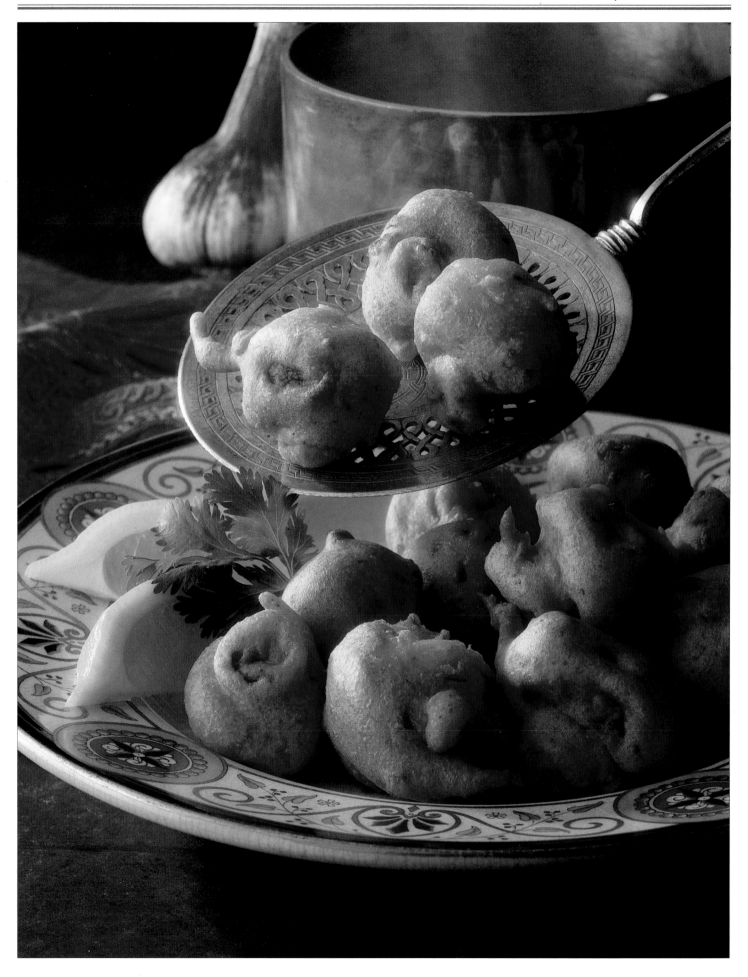

Pakoras

These vegetable fritters are simple to make and extremely good to eat. They may be served as a tasty starter or as an accompaniment to a main course.

SERVES 4–6

INGREDIENTS

4 oz broccoli
1 onion
2 potatoes
1½ cups gram flour
1 tsp garam masala
1½ tsp salt
½ tsp cayenne pepper
1 tsp cumin seeds
scant 1 cup water
vegetable oil, for deep-frying
sprigs of cilantro, to garnish

1 Cut the broccoli into small flowerets, discarding most of the stalk, and cook in a pan of boiling, salted water for 4 minutes. Drain well, return to the pan, and shake dry over a low heat for a few moments. Place the broccoli on absorbent paper towels to completely dry while preparing the other vegetables.

2 Peel and thinly slice the onion and separate into rings. Peel and thinly slice the potatoes and pat dry.

3 Place the gram flour in a bowl with the garam masala, salt, cayenne pepper, and cumin seeds. Make a well in the center, add the water, and then mix to form a smooth batter.

4 One-third fill a deep fat fryer or pan with oil and heat to 375°F or until a cube of day-old bread browns in 30 seconds. Dip the vegetables into the batter to coat, then lower into the hot oil, and fry, in batches, for 3–4 minutes or until golden brown and crisp. Drain on absorbent paper towels and keep warm while cooking the remainder in the same way. Serve the pakoras hot, garnished with sprigs of cilantro.

Step *1*

Step *4*

Step *4*

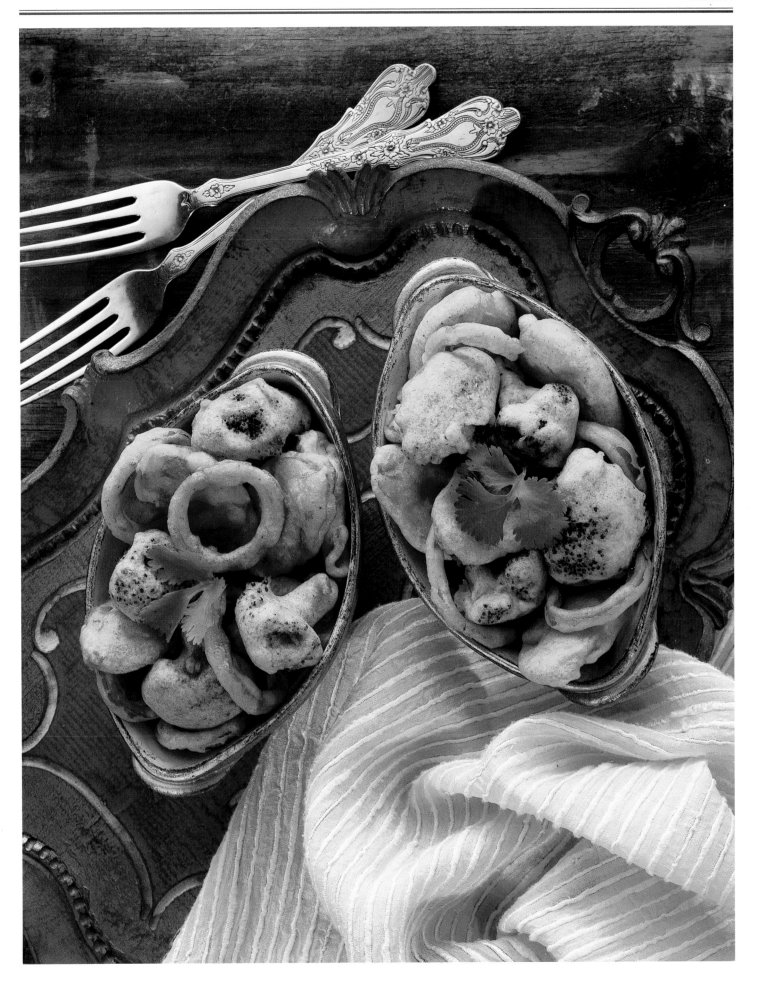

Vegetable & Cashew Samosas

These delicious little fried pastries are really quite simple to make. Serve them hot as a starter to an Indian meal or cold as a tasty picnic or lunchtime snack.

MAKES 12

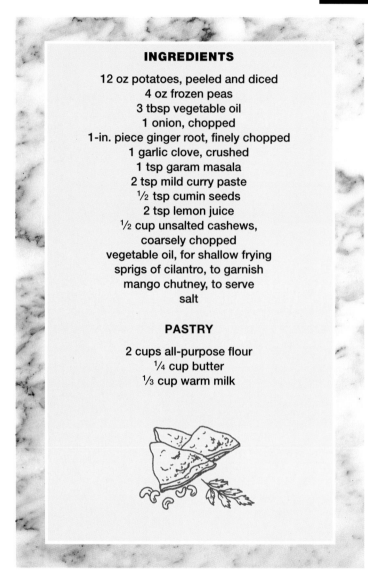

INGREDIENTS

12 oz potatoes, peeled and diced
4 oz frozen peas
3 tbsp vegetable oil
1 onion, chopped
1-in. piece ginger root, finely chopped
1 garlic clove, crushed
1 tsp garam masala
2 tsp mild curry paste
½ tsp cumin seeds
2 tsp lemon juice
½ cup unsalted cashews,
coarsely chopped
vegetable oil, for shallow frying
sprigs of cilantro, to garnish
mango chutney, to serve
salt

PASTRY

2 cups all-purpose flour
¼ cup butter
⅓ cup warm milk

1 Cook the potatoes in a saucepan of boiling, salted water for 5 minutes. Add the peas and cook for a further 4 minutes or until the potato is tender. Drain well. Heat the oil in a skillet, add the onion, potato and pea mixture, ginger, garlic, and spices, and fry for 2 minutes. Stir in the lemon juice and cook gently, uncovered, for 2 minutes. Remove from the heat, slightly mash the potato and peas, then add the cashews, mix well, and season with salt.

2 To make the pastry, put the flour in a bowl and rub in the butter finely. Mix in the milk to form a dough. Knead lightly and divide into 6 portions. Form each into a ball and roll out on a lightly floured counter to a 7 in. round. Cut each one in half.

3 Divide the filling equally between each semi-circle of dough, spreading it out to within ¼ in. of the edges. Brush the edges of the dough all the way round with water and fold over to form triangular shapes, sealing the edges well together to enclose the filling completely.

4 One-third fill a large, deep skillet with oil and heat to 350°F or until hot enough to brown a cube of bread in 30 seconds. Fry the samosas, a few at a time, turning frequently until golden brown and heated through. Drain on paper towels and keep warm while cooking the remainder in the same way. Garnish with sprigs of cilantro and serve hot.

Step *2*

Step *3*

Step *4*

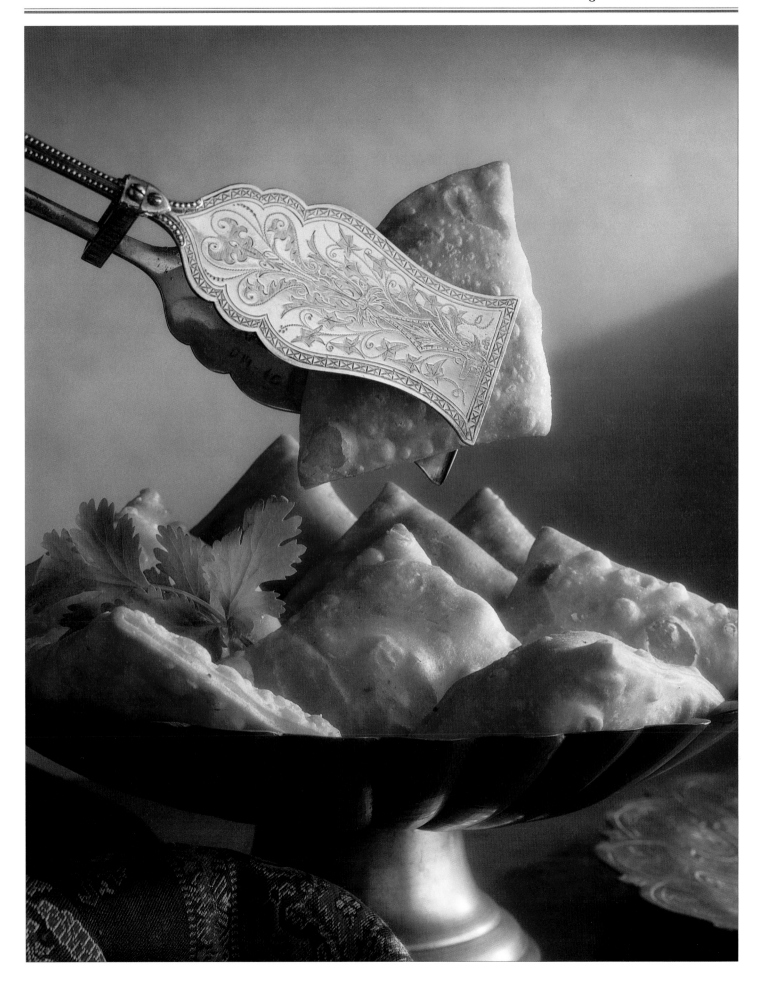

Spiced Chicken Koftas with Lime Pickle

Koftas are spicy meatballs. In this recipe they are made with chicken, but you could use lamb or beef. Lime pickle is available in Asian food stores and some supermarkets.

SERVES 4

INGREDIENTS

1lb skinned and boned chicken, chopped coarsely
1 garlic clove
1-in. piece ginger root, grated
4 tsp garam masala
½ tsp ground turmeric
2 tbsp chopped fresh cilantro
½ green bell pepper, chopped coarsely
2 fresh green chilies, deseeded
½ tsp salt
6 tbsp oil
1 jar lime pickle, to serve
lime wedges, to garnish

1 Put all the ingredients, except the oil, lime pickle, and lime wedges into a food processor or blender and process until the mixture is chopped finely. Alternatively, finely chop the chicken, garlic, ginger, bell pepper, and chilies, and mix together in a bowl with the garam masala, turmeric, cilantro, and salt.

2 Shape the mixture into 16 small balls.

3 Heat the oil in a karahi or wok and fry the koftas for 8–10 minutes, turning them occasionally to ensure they cook evenly. If you cannot fit all the koftas into the pan at once, keep the first batch warm in a low oven, while you fry the remaining koftas.

4 Drain the koftas on paper towels and serve hot with lime pickle and garnished with lime wedges.

Step *1*

Step *2*

Step *3*

Rashmi Kebabs

This is a variation on Sheek Kebab. A little attention is needed when making the egg 'nets', but the extra effort is worth it, as the effect is very impressive.

SERVES 4

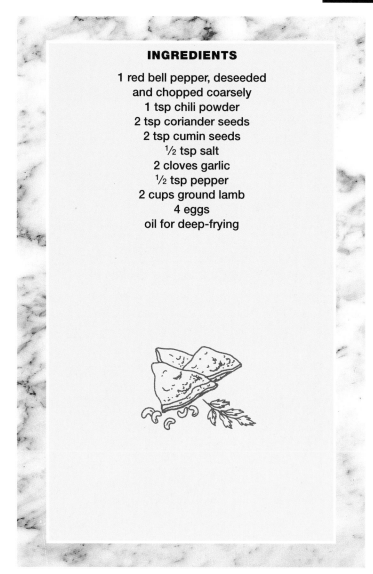

INGREDIENTS

1 red bell pepper, deseeded
and chopped coarsely
1 tsp chili powder
2 tsp coriander seeds
2 tsp cumin seeds
½ tsp salt
2 cloves garlic
½ tsp pepper
2 cups ground lamb
4 eggs
oil for deep-frying

1 Grind the red bell pepper, chili powder, coriander seeds, cumin seeds, salt, garlic, and black pepper in a food processor or blender. Alternatively, pound the coriander and cumin with a pestle and mortar, chop the red bell pepper and garlic very finely, and mix with the ground spices, salt, chili powder, and black pepper.

2 Transfer the spice mixture to a bowl and add the lamb and 1 of the eggs. Mix well to evenly distribute the egg and bind the mixture together.

3 Divide the lamb mixture into 8. Shape 1 piece into a ball. Put the ball on a clean plate and gently squash the top with the palm of your hand, to form a patty. Repeat with the remaining pieces. If possible, refrigerate the kebabs for at least 30 minutes.

4 Cook the kebabs under a preheated hot broiler for 15 minutes, turning once.

5 Meanwhile, make the egg nets. Beat together the remaining eggs. Fill a large skillet with oil to a depth of 2–3 inches. Heat until a cube of bread that is dropped in sizzles in 1 minute.

6 Trickle the egg off the end of a spoon into the oil, crisscrossing the lines in a grid shape. It will take only seconds to cook. Remove and drain on plenty of paper towels. Repeat until all the egg is used. Wrap each kebab in 1–2 egg nets. Serve warm.

Step *1*

Step *2*

Step *6*

Lamb & Tomato Koftas

These little meatballs, served with a minty yogurt dressing, can be prepared well in advance, ready to cook when required.

SERVES 4

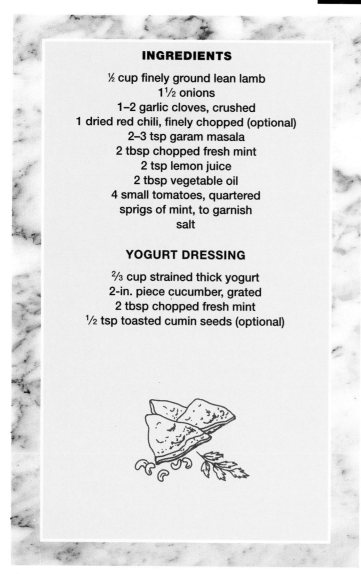

INGREDIENTS

½ cup finely ground lean lamb
1½ onions
1–2 garlic cloves, crushed
1 dried red chili, finely chopped (optional)
2–3 tsp garam masala
2 tbsp chopped fresh mint
2 tsp lemon juice
2 tbsp vegetable oil
4 small tomatoes, quartered
sprigs of mint, to garnish
salt

YOGURT DRESSING

⅔ cup strained thick yogurt
2-in. piece cucumber, grated
2 tbsp chopped fresh mint
½ tsp toasted cumin seeds (optional)

1 Place the ground lamb in a bowl. Finely chop 1 onion and add to the bowl with the garlic and chili, if using. Stir in the garam masala, mint, and lemon juice and season well with salt. Mix the ingredients well together.

2 Divide the mixture in half, then divide each half into 10 equal portions, and form each into a small ball. Roll the balls in the oil to coat. Quarter the remaining onion half and separate into layers.

3 Thread 5 of the balls, 4 tomato quarters, and some of the onion layers onto each of 4 bamboo or metal skewers. Brush the vegetables with the remaining oil and cook under a hot broiler for about 10 minutes, turning frequently until they are browned all over and cooked through.

4 Meanwhile, prepare the yogurt dressing. Mix the yogurt with the cucumber, mint, and toasted cumin seeds, if using. Garnish the lamb koftas with sprigs of mint and serve hot with the yogurt dressing.

Step *1*

Step *2*

Step *3*

Sheek Kebabs

*Sheek Kebabs are delicious cooked over a barbecue. Serve in pitta bread
for great party food. The cooked meat can also be chopped into a salad.*

SERVES 4-8

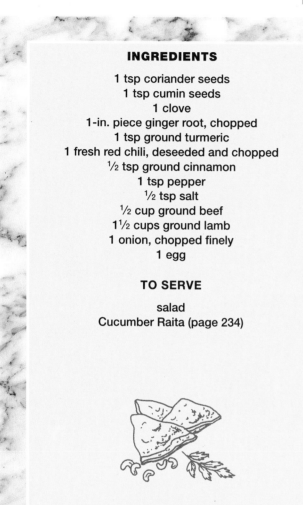

INGREDIENTS

1 tsp coriander seeds
1 tsp cumin seeds
1 clove
1-in. piece ginger root, chopped
1 tsp ground turmeric
1 fresh red chili, deseeded and chopped
½ tsp ground cinnamon
1 tsp pepper
½ tsp salt
½ cup ground beef
1½ cups ground lamb
1 onion, chopped finely
1 egg

TO SERVE

salad
Cucumber Raita (page 234)

1 Pound together the coriander, cumin, clove, and ginger with a pestle and mortar. Mix in the turmeric, chili, cinnamon, pepper, and salt.

2 Combine the spice mixture with the beef, lamb, and onion.

3 Make a well in the center of the meat mixture, add the egg, and mix in thoroughly.

4 Press one-eighth of the meat mixture around an oiled skewer, to form a shape about 4 inches long and 1 in. thick. Repeat with the remaining meat mixture.

5 If possible, leave to rest in the refrigerator for at least 1 hour.

6 Cook the kebabs under a preheated medium broiler for about 20 minutes, turning once or twice, until the meat juices run clear when the thickest part of the meatballs is pierced with the point of a sharp knife.

7 Serve with salad and cucumber raita.

Step *1*

Step *3*

Step *4*

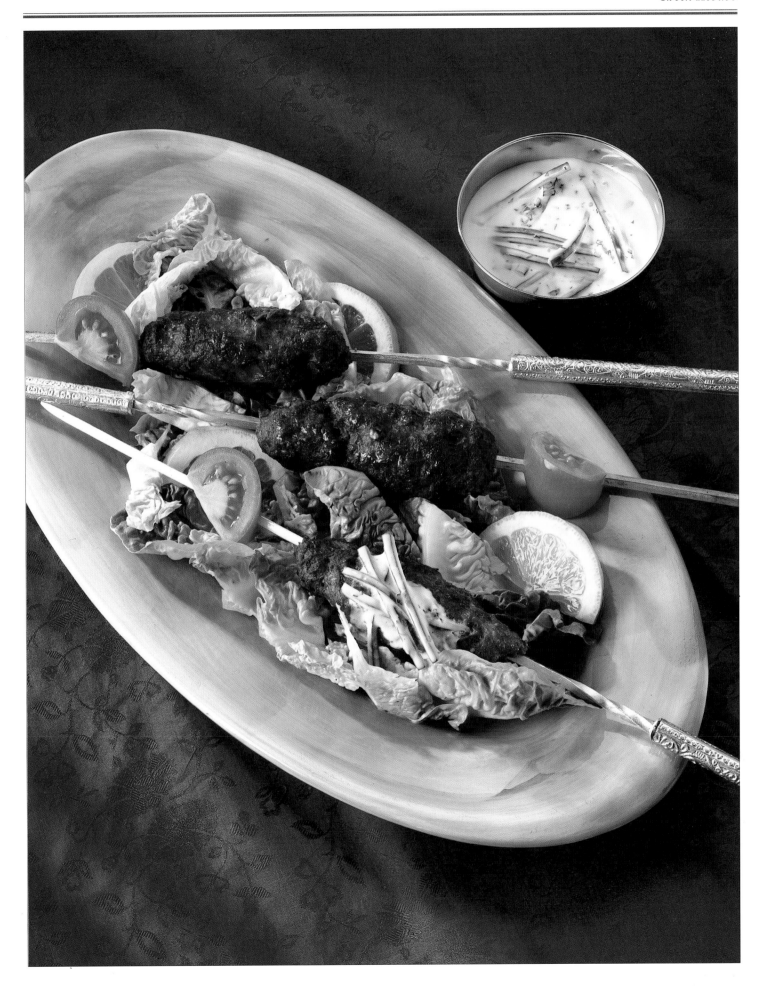

Masala Kebabs

Indian kebab dishes are not necessarily cooked on a skewer; they can also be served in a dish and are always dry dishes with no sauce.

SERVES 4–6

INGREDIENTS

1 dried bay leaf
1-in. piece ginger root, chopped
1 in. cinnamon stick
1 tsp coriander seeds
½ tsp salt
1 tsp fennel seeds
1 tsp chili powder
1 tsp garam masala
1 tsp lemon juice
1 tsp ground turmeric
1 tbsp oil
1½ lb lamb neck fillet

TO GARNISH

sprigs of fresh cilantro
lemon wedges

TO SERVE

bread
chutney

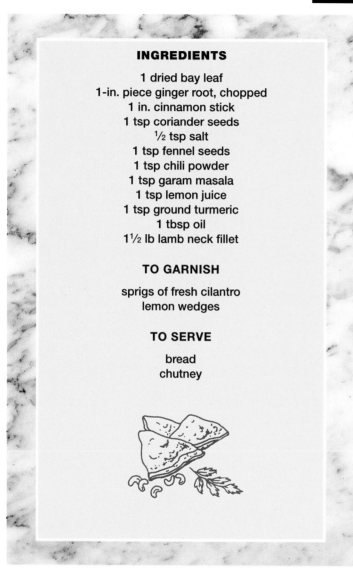

1 Use a food processor, blender, or pestle and mortar to grind together the bay leaf, ginger, cinnamon, coriander seeds, salt, fennel seeds, and chili powder.

2 Combine this spice mix with the garam masala, lemon juice, turmeric, and oil in a large bowl.

3 Cut the lamb into ¼ in. slices.

4 Add to the spice mix and leave to marinate at room temperature for about 1 hour, or in the refrigerator for 3 hours or overnight.

5 Spread out the pieces of lamb on a cookie sheet and cook in a preheated oven, 400°F, for 20 minutes until well done. Transfer to paper towels to drain any excess fat.

6 Thread 3 or 4 pieces of meat onto each skewer and garnish with sprigs of fresh cilantro and lemon wedges. Serve hot with bread and chutney.

Step *1*

Step *3*

Step *5*

FISH DISHES

At first glance India may not be considered a great fish-eating nation, but India has a coastline stretching for over 2,500 miles, and with internal waters can supply over 2,000 varieties of fish!

Fish is very popular in some areas and plays an important part in the diet. There is a vast array of fresh seafood in southern India, Bengal, Calcutta and its environs, and as far north as Darjeeling. North of Calcutta rivers and streams flow from the Himalayas. The water is very clean and pure, and a great variety of river fish is caught. Lake fish are also enjoyed when available.

Many fish and shellfish are simply broiled, whole or on skewers, after sprinkling with a few spices and brushing with mustard oil. Others are fried whole or as fish and vegetable fritters. Fish with a firm, meaty texture, like cod, are curried in aromatic sauces and frequently flavored with coconut. Countless others are baked, steamed, poached, or roasted with that characteristic Indian flavor that is based on a masala of spices that enhances, but does not overwhelm, the delicate flavor of the fish.

Indian Broiled Trout

Here is a deliciously simple way of preparing and cooking trout.
It is also good with nice fresh, plump mackerel.

SERVES 4

INGREDIENTS

4 trout, about 8 oz
6 tbsp ghee or melted butter
1–2 garlic cloves, peeled and crushed
1 fresh green chili, deseeded and chopped,
or 1 tsp ground chili (from a jar)
1-in. piece ginger root,
peeled and chopped finely
1½ tsp cumin seeds
1 tsp garam masala
1 tsp ground cumin
finely grated rind of 1 lemon
juice of 2 lemons
salt

TO GARNISH

sprigs of cilantro
lemon wedges

1 Using a sharp knife, carefully make 3 diagonal slashes (not too deep) on each side of the trout. Season the trout and place in a lightly greased broiler pan.

2 Heat the ghee or butter in a small pan over a low heat, add the crushed garlic, chili, chopped ginger, and spices and cook very gently for 30 seconds, stirring.

3 Remove the pan from the heat and stir the lemon rind and juice into the mixture.

4 Spoon half the mixture over the trout and cook under a moderately hot broiler for 5–8 minutes or until cooked on one side. Turn the fish over, spoon the remaining mixture over the fish, and broil for a further 5–8 minutes, basting frequently with the juices in the pan during cooking.

5 Arrange the trout on a hot serving plate, spoon the pan juices over the fish, and garnish with sprigs of cilantro and lemon wedges. Serve hot.

Step *1*

Step *3*

Step *4*

Indian Cod with Tomatoes

Quick and easy – cod steaks are cooked in a rich tomato and coconut sauce to produce tender, succulent results.

SERVES 4

INGREDIENTS

3 tbsp vegetable oil
4 cod steaks, about 1 in. thick
1 onion, chopped finely
2 garlic cloves, crushed
1 red bell pepper, deseeded and chopped
1 tsp ground coriander
1 tsp ground cumin
1 tsp ground turmeric
½ tsp garam masala
14 oz can chopped tomatoes
⅔ cup coconut milk
1–2 tbsp chopped fresh cilantro
or parsley
salt and pepper

1 Heat the oil in a skillet, add the fish steaks, season with salt and pepper, and fry until browned on both sides (but not cooked through). Remove from the skillet and reserve.

2 Add the onion, garlic, red bell pepper, and spices and cook very gently for 2 minutes, stirring frequently. Add the tomatoes, bring to a boil, and simmer for 5 minutes.

3 Return the fish steaks to the skillet and simmer gently for 8 minutes or until the fish is cooked through. Remove the fish from the skillet and keep warm on a serving dish.

4 Add the coconut milk and cilantro to the pan and reheat gently. Spoon the sauce over the cod steaks and serve immediately.

Step *2*

Step *3*

Step *4*

Masala Fried Fish

Frying fish is classically Indian, although it does not always spring to mind when thinking of Indian food.

SERVES 4–8

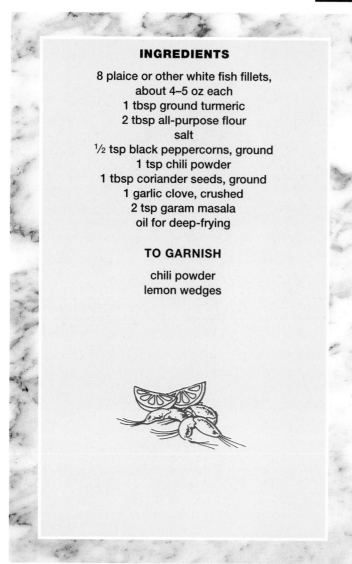

INGREDIENTS

8 plaice or other white fish fillets,
about 4–5 oz each
1 tbsp ground turmeric
2 tbsp all-purpose flour
salt
½ tsp black peppercorns, ground
1 tsp chili powder
1 tbsp coriander seeds, ground
1 garlic clove, crushed
2 tsp garam masala
oil for deep-frying

TO GARNISH

chili powder
lemon wedges

1 To skin the fish fillets, lay the fillet skin side down with the tail nearest you. Hold the tail end between your thumb and forefinger. Hold a sharp knife at a shallow angle to the fish in your other hand. Holding the fish firmly, make an angled cut between the flesh and the skin, then continue to cut the flesh away from the skin until it is free.

2 In a shallow dish, combine the turmeric, flour, salt, peppercorns, chili powder, coriander seeds, garlic, and garam masala. Mix well.

3 Fill a shallow saucepan or a deep skillet with oil to a depth of 2–3 inches, and heat to 350° F.

4 Coat the fish fillets in the spice mix either by shaking gently in a paper bag or turning over in the dish of spice mix until well coated.

5 Deep-fry the fish fillets for about 3–5 minutes, turning often, until the flesh flakes with a fork. Drain on plenty of paper towels.

6 Serve sprinkled with chili powder, garnished with lemon wedges, and accompanied by a selection of pickles and chutneys.

Step *1*

Step *2*

Step *5*

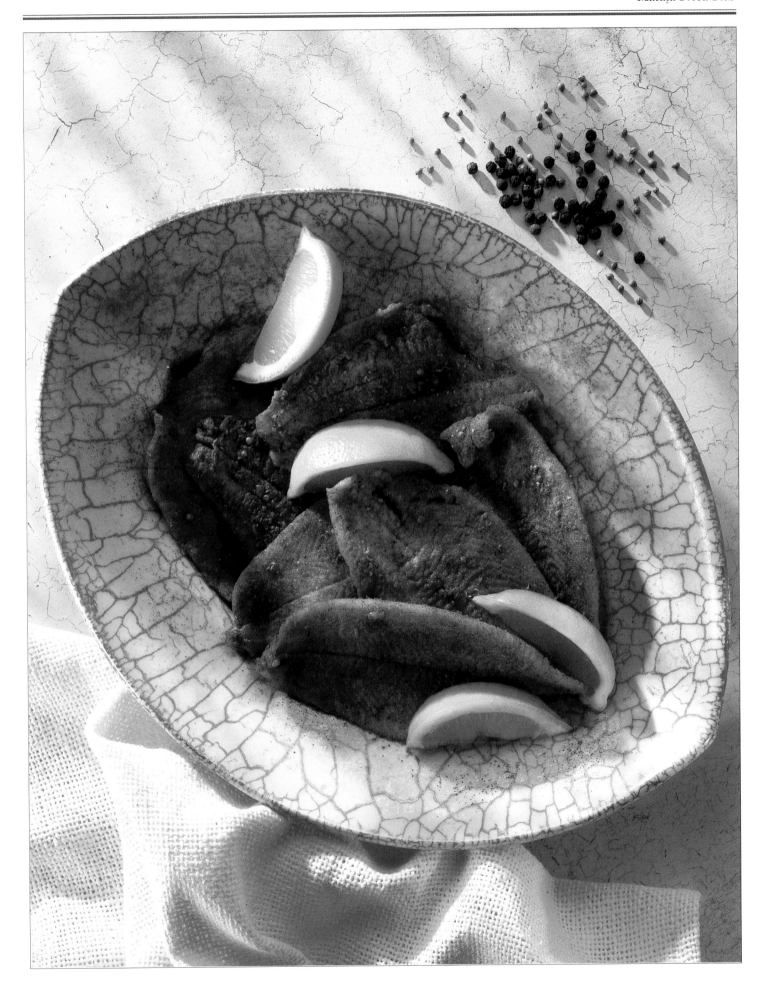

Spicy Fish & Potato Fritters

You need nice, floury-textured main crop potatoes for making these tasty fritters. Any white fish of your choice may be used.

SERVES 4

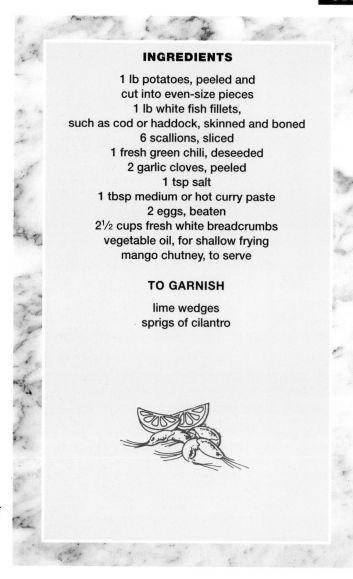

INGREDIENTS

1 lb potatoes, peeled and
cut into even-size pieces
1 lb white fish fillets,
such as cod or haddock, skinned and boned
6 scallions, sliced
1 fresh green chili, deseeded
2 garlic cloves, peeled
1 tsp salt
1 tbsp medium or hot curry paste
2 eggs, beaten
2½ cups fresh white breadcrumbs
vegetable oil, for shallow frying
mango chutney, to serve

TO GARNISH

lime wedges
sprigs of cilantro

1 Cook the potatoes in a pan of boiling, salted water until tender. Drain well, return the potatoes to the pan, and place over a moderate heat for a few moments to dry off. Cool slightly, then place in a food processor with the fish, onions, chili, garlic, salt, and curry paste. Process until the ingredients are very finely chopped and blended.

2 Turn the potato mixture into a bowl and mix in 2 tablespoons of beaten egg, and 1 cup of breadcrumbs. Place the remaining beaten egg and breadcrumbs in separate dishes.

3 Divide the fish mixture into 8 and, using a spoon to help you (the mixture is quite soft), dip first in the beaten egg, and then coat in the breadcrumbs, and carefully shape the mixture into ovals.

4 Heat enough oil in a large skillet for shallow frying and fry the fritters over moderate heat for 3–4 minutes, turning frequently, until golden brown and cooked through. Drain on absorbent paper towels and garnish with lime wedges and sprigs of cilantro. Serve hot, with mango chutney.

Step *2*

Step *3*

Step *4*

Deep-Fried Battered Fish

*The crispy, spicy battered fish is complemented by a tangy fenugreek
dip. The dish makes a delicious and light start to a meal.*

SERVES 4

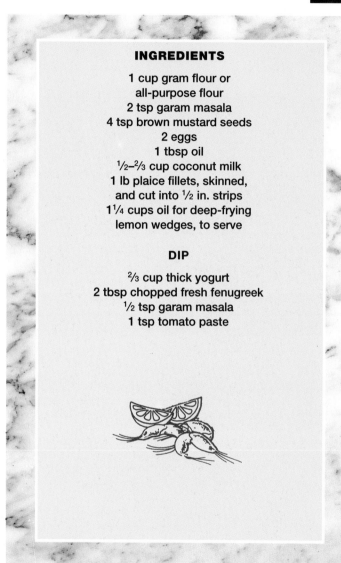

INGREDIENTS

1 cup gram flour or
all-purpose flour
2 tsp garam masala
4 tsp brown mustard seeds
2 eggs
1 tbsp oil
½–⅔ cup coconut milk
1 lb plaice fillets, skinned,
and cut into ½ in. strips
1¼ cups oil for deep-frying
lemon wedges, to serve

DIP

⅔ cup thick yogurt
2 tbsp chopped fresh fenugreek
½ tsp garam masala
1 tsp tomato paste

1 Sift the flour into a bowl and add the garam masala and mustard seeds. Make a well in the center and gradually add the eggs, 1 tablespoon of oil, and enough coconut milk to make a batter which has the consistency of thick cream.

2 Coat the fish in the batter and set aside.

3 To make the dip, put the yogurt, fenugreek, garam masala, and tomato paste into a bowl and mix together.

4 Heat the oil in a karahi or wok. Add the fish in batches so the pan is not crowded, and deep-fry for 3–4 minutes until golden brown. Transfer the fish to paper towels to drain, then keep warm in a low oven while you cook the rest of the fish.

5 Serve the fish hot with lemon wedges and the dip.

Step *1*

Step *3*

Step *4*

Green Fish Curry

This dish is from southern India. It has a wonderful fresh, hot, exotic taste resulting from the generous amount of fresh herbs, sharp fresh chilies, and coconut milk.

SERVES 4

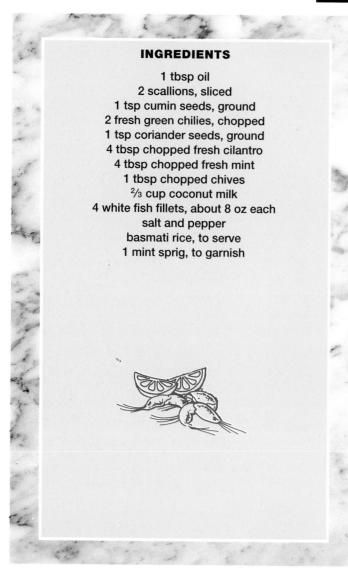

INGREDIENTS

1 tbsp oil
2 scallions, sliced
1 tsp cumin seeds, ground
2 fresh green chilies, chopped
1 tsp coriander seeds, ground
4 tbsp chopped fresh cilantro
4 tbsp chopped fresh mint
1 tbsp chopped chives
²/₃ cup coconut milk
4 white fish fillets, about 8 oz each
salt and pepper
basmati rice, to serve
1 mint sprig, to garnish

1 Heat the oil in a large skillet or shallow saucepan and add the scallions.

2 Stir-fry the scallions over a medium heat until they are softened but not colored. Stir in the cumin, chilies, and ground coriander, and cook them until fragrant.

3 Add the fresh cilantro, mint, chives, and coconut milk and season liberally.

4 Carefully place the fish in the skillet or pan and poach for 10–15 minutes until the flesh flakes when tested with a fork.

5 Serve the fish fillets in the sauce with basmati rice and garnish with a sprig of mint.

Step *2*

Step *3*

Step *4*

Shrimp Curry & Fruit Sauce

Serve this lightly-spiced dish as part of a buffet meal, or as a refreshingly different lunch dish, with rice or poppadoms.

SERVES 4

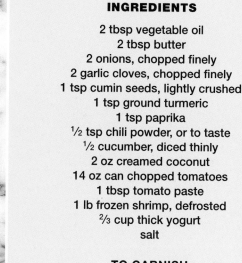

INGREDIENTS

2 tbsp vegetable oil
2 tbsp butter
2 onions, chopped finely
2 garlic cloves, chopped finely
1 tsp cumin seeds, lightly crushed
1 tsp ground turmeric
1 tsp paprika
½ tsp chili powder, or to taste
½ cucumber, diced thinly
2 oz creamed coconut
14 oz can chopped tomatoes
1 tbsp tomato paste
1 lb frozen shrimp, defrosted
⅔ cup thick yogurt
salt

TO GARNISH

2 hard-cooked eggs, quartered
sprigs of cilantro
onion rings

FRUIT SAUCE

1¼ cups natural yogurt
¼ tsp salt
1 garlic clove, crushed
2 tbsp fresh mint, chopped
4 tbsp seedless raisins
1 small pomegranate

1 Heat the oil and butter in a skillet. Add the chopped onions and fry until translucent. Add the garlic and fry for a further minute, until softened but not browned.

2 Stir in the cumin seeds, turmeric, paprika, and chili powder and cook for 2 minutes, stirring. Stir in the creamed coconut, chopped tomatoes, and tomato paste and bring to a boil. Simmer for 10 minutes, or until the sauce has thickened slightly. It should not be at all runny.

3 Remove the skillet from the heat and set aside to cool. Stir in the shrimp, cucumber, and yogurt. Taste the sauce and adjust the seasoning if necessary. Cover and chill until ready to serve.

4 To make the fruit sauce, place the yogurt in a bowl and stir in the salt, garlic, mint, and raisins. Cut the pomegranate in half, scoop out the seeds, and discard the white membrane. Stir the seeds into the yogurt, reserving a few for garnish.

5 Transfer the curry to a serving dish and arrange the hard-cooked egg, cilantro, and onion rings on top. Serve the sauce separately, sprinkled with the reserved pomegranate seeds.

Step *1*

Step *2*

Step *3*

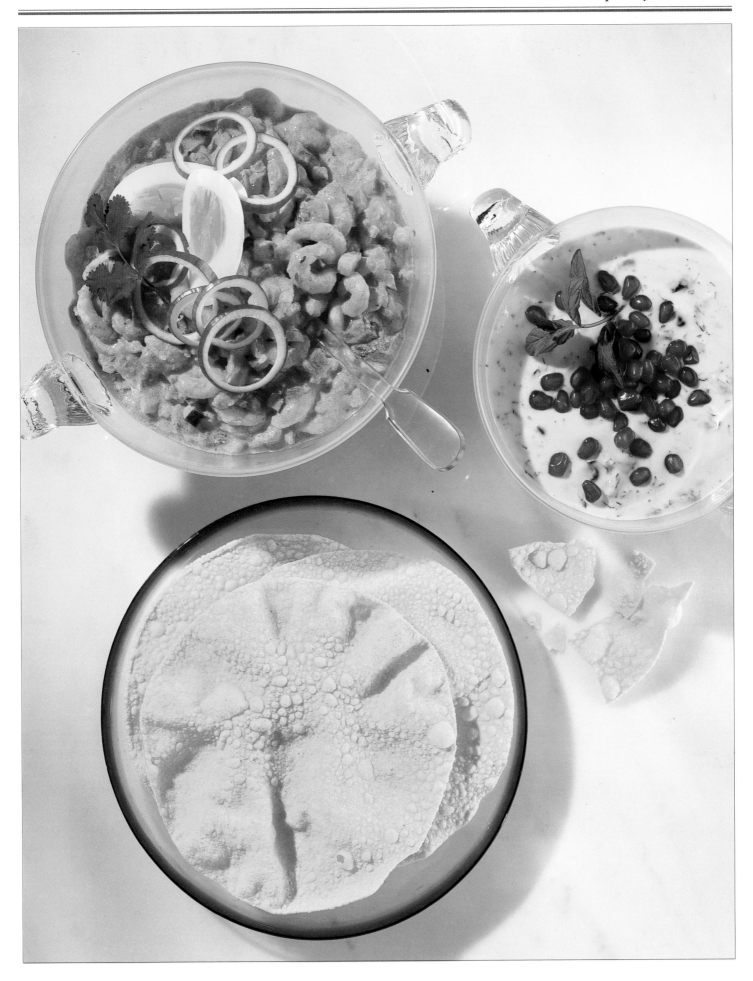

Curried Crab

Shellfish is a major part of the diet in coastal areas of India. It is frozen and shipped to all parts India, to be used in a wide variety of dishes.

SERVES 4

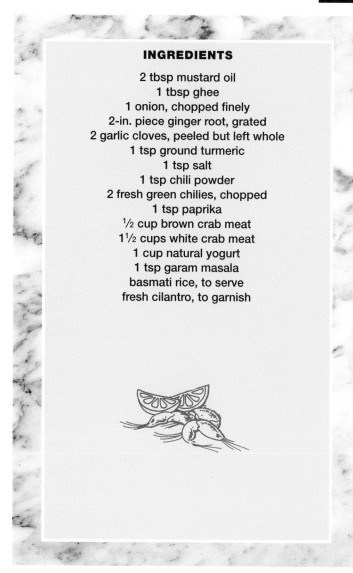

INGREDIENTS

2 tbsp mustard oil
1 tbsp ghee
1 onion, chopped finely
2-in. piece ginger root, grated
2 garlic cloves, peeled but left whole
1 tsp ground turmeric
1 tsp salt
1 tsp chili powder
2 fresh green chilies, chopped
1 tsp paprika
½ cup brown crab meat
1½ cups white crab meat
1 cup natural yogurt
1 tsp garam masala
basmati rice, to serve
fresh cilantro, to garnish

1 Heat the mustard oil in a large, preferably non-stick, skillet, wok, or saucepan. When it starts to smoke. add the ghee and onion. Stir for 3 minutes over a medium heat until the onion is soft.

2 Stir in the ginger and whole garlic cloves.

3 Add the turmeric, salt, chili powder, chilies, and paprika. Mix thoroughly.

4 Increase the heat and add the crab meat and yogurt. Simmer, stirring occasionally, for 10 minutes until the sauce is thickened slightly. Add garam masala to taste.

5 Serve hot, over plain basmati rice, with the fresh cilantro either chopped or in sprigs.

Step *1*

Step *2*

Step *3*

Shrimp & Chili Sauce

Quick and easy to prepare and extremely good to eat. Use the large and succulent tiger shrimp for special occasions.

SERVES 4

INGREDIENTS

4 tbsp ghee or vegetable oil
1 onion, quartered and sliced
1 bunch scallions,
trimmed and sliced
1 garlic clove, crushed
1–2 fresh green chilies,
deseeded and finely chopped
1-in. piece ginger root,
finely chopped
1 tsp ground turmeric
1 tsp ground cumin
1 tsp ground coriander
1½ tsp curry powder or paste
14 oz can chopped tomatoes
⅔ cup water
⅔ cup heavy cream
1 lb peeled shrimp
1–2 tbsp chopped fresh cilantro
salt
sprigs of cilantro, to garnish

1 Heat the ghee or vegetable oil in a saucepan and fry the onions, garlic, and chili over gentle heat for 3 minutes. Stir in the ginger, spices, and curry powder or paste and cook very gently for a further 1 minute, stirring all the time.

2 Stir in the tomatoes and water and bring to a boil, stirring. Reduce the heat and simmer for 10 minutes, stirring occasionally.

3 Add the cream, mix well, and simmer for 5 minutes, then add the shrimp and cilantro, and season with salt to taste. Cook gently for 2–3 minutes. Taste and adjust the seasoning, if necessary. Serve garnished with sprigs of cilantro.

Step *1*

Step *2*

Step *3*

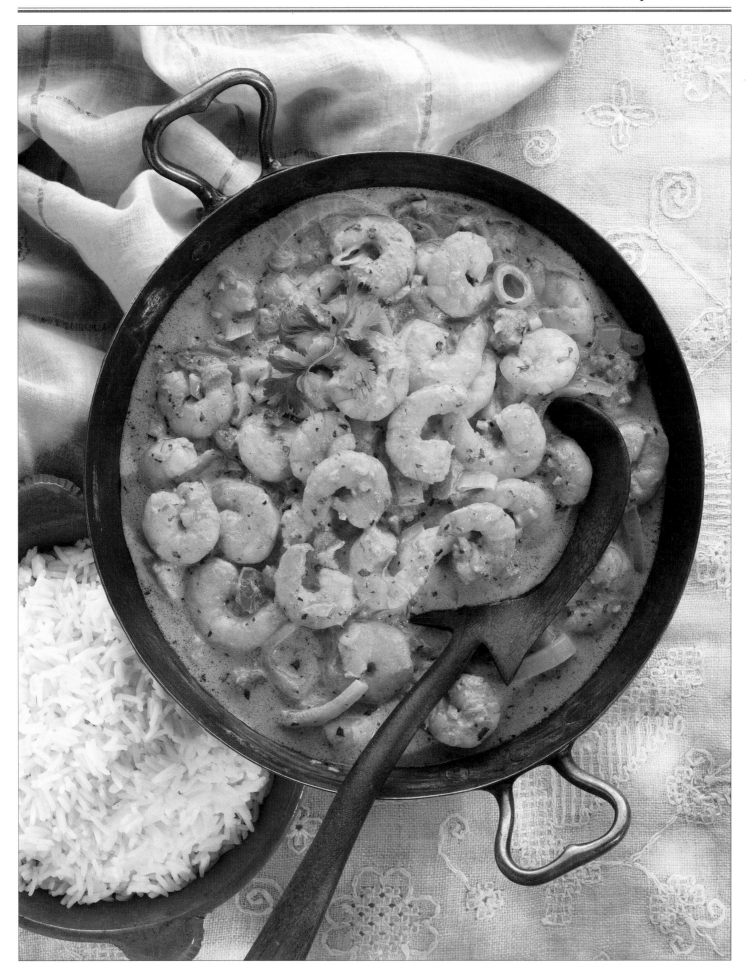

Balti Jumbo Shrimp

Although shrimp are not a traditional ingredient of Balti cooking, they work well with Balti spices and Balti cooking methods.

SERVES 4

INGREDIENTS

1 garlic clove, crushed
2 tsp freshly grated ginger root
2 tsp ground coriander
2 tsp ground cumin
½ tsp ground cardamom
¼ tsp chili powder
2 tbsp tomato paste
5 tbsp water
3 tbsp chopped fresh cilantro
1 lb peeled cooked jumbo shrimp
2 tbsp oil
2 small onions, sliced
1 fresh green chili, chopped
salt

1 Put the garlic, ginger, ground coriander, cumin, cardamom, chili powder, tomato paste, 4 tablespoons of the water, and 2 tablespoons of the fresh cilantro into a bowl. Mix all the ingredients together.

2 Add the shrimp to the bowl and leave to marinate for 2 hours.

3 Heat the oil in a karahi or wok, add the onions, and stir-fry until golden brown.

4 Add the shrimp, marinade, and the chili and stir-fry over a medium heat for 5 minutes. Add salt, and the remaining tablespoon of water if the mixture is very dry. Stir-fry over a medium heat for a further 5 minutes.

5 Serve immediately with the remaining fresh chopped cilantro.

Step *1*

Step *3*

Step *4*

Shrimp Dansak

The lentil purée sauce in this recipe is of Parsi origin and is popular throughout the whole of India.

SERVES 4–6

INGREDIENTS

1½ lb uncooked tiger shrimp
in their shells or 1 lb 5 oz
peeled tiger shrimp, cooked
1 tsp salt
1 bay leaf
3 garlic cloves
⅓ cup split yellow peas,
soaked for 1 hour in cold water and drained
¼ cup red lentils
1 carrot, chopped
1 potato, cut into large dice
3 tbsp drained canned corn
3 tbsp oil
2 onions, chopped
½ tsp yellow mustard seeds
1½ tsp coriander seeds, ground
½ tsp cumin seeds, ground
½ tsp fenugreek seeds, ground
1½ tsp ground turmeric
1 dried red chili
14 oz can tomatoes
½ tsp garam masala
3 tbsp chopped fresh cilantro
2 tbsp chopped fresh mint

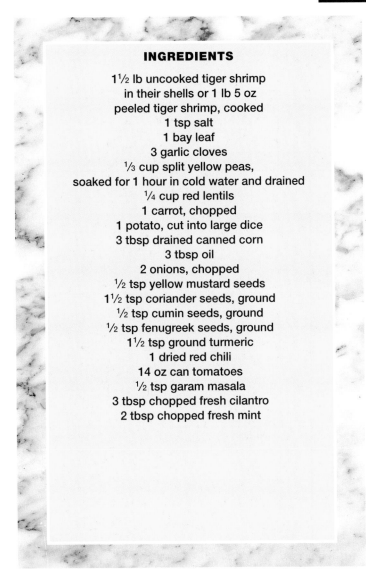

1 Reserve a few of the shrimp for garnish and peel the rest. Set aside. Cook those for the garnish in boiling water for 3–5 minutes if not already cooked.

2 Fill a large saucepan with water and add the salt, bay leaf, 1 garlic clove, and the split yellow peas. Bring to a boil and cook for 15 minutes. Add the red lentils, carrot, and potato and cook, uncovered, for a further 15 minutes. Drain, discarding the garlic and bay leaf.

3 Purée the cooked vegetables with the corn in a blender or food processor. Alternatively, use a potato masher to break down the lumps.

4 Crush the remaining garlic. Heat the oil in a large saucepan and cook the onion and garlic for 3–4 minutes. Add the mustard seeds and when they start to pop, stir in the coriander, cumin and fenugreek seeds, turmeric and chili. Add the shrimp and stir over a high heat for 1–2 minutes.

5 Add the tomatoes and the puréed vegetables, and gently simmer. Cook, uncovered, for 30–40 minutes. Stir in the garam masala and taste for seasoning.

6 Serve, sprinkled with the fresh cilantro and mint, and garnished with the reserved shrimp.

Step *1*

Step *3*

Step *4*

Shrimp Bhuna

This is a fiery recipe with subtle undertones. As the flavor of the shrimp should be noticeable, the spices should not take over this dish.

SERVES 4–6

INGREDIENTS

2 dried red chilies, deseeded if liked
3 fresh green chilies, finely chopped
1 tsp ground turmeric
2 tsp white wine vinegar
½ tsp salt
3 garlic cloves, crushed
½ tsp pepper
1 tsp paprika
1 lb uncooked peeled jumbo shrimp
4 tbsp oil
1 onion, chopped very finely
¾ cup water
2 tbsp lemon juice
2 tsp garam masala
sprigs of fresh cilantro, to garnish

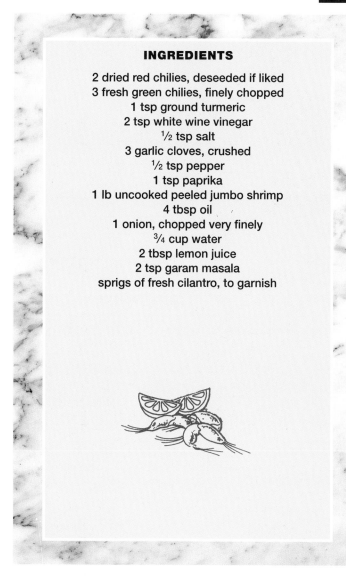

1 Combine the chilies, turmeric, vinegar, salt, garlic, pepper, and paprika in a non-metallic bowl. Stir in the shrimp and set aside for 10 minutes.

2 Heat the oil in a large skillet or wok, add the onion, and fry for 3–4 minutes until soft.

3 Add the shrimp and the contents of the bowl to the pan and stir-fry over a high heat for 2 minutes.

4 Reduce the heat, add the water, and boil for 10 minutes, stirring occasionally, until the water is evaporated and the curry is fragrant.

5 Stir in the lemon juice and garam masala.

6 Serve garnished with sprigs of fresh cilantro.

Step *1*

Step *3*

Step *4*

POULTRY DISHES

Chicken is probably one of the most frequently used meats in Indian cooking, particularly in northern India where milder dishes are a specialty and dairy products more prevalent. The delicate flavor and texture of chicken combines well with richly-flavored aromatic sauces based on yogurt, cream, and ground nuts which bring to mind the opulent days of the maharajahs and nazirs of long-ago India.
These sauces have a subtle balance of flavors and spice mixes, and extra chili should not be added to heat them up. As it does not take long to cook, chicken lends itself well to the quick stir-fry cooking method, or it can be quickly roasted tandoori-style. You can either buy whole chickens and joint them yourself, or buy chicken pieces, or, for convenience, use boneless chicken breasts. As in many Asian countries, the chickens used in India are often free-range and scrawny, but they have a flavor far superior to the battery-raised birds of the West. Marinating the chicken for as long as possible really helps to give it a more interesting flavor.

Tandoori Chicken

To replicate the intense heat of a traditional tandoor oven, cook the tandoori chicken at a very high temperature, preferably on a barbecue.

SERVES 4

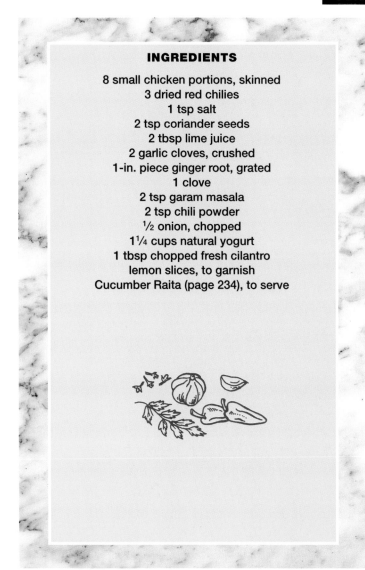

INGREDIENTS

8 small chicken portions, skinned
3 dried red chilies
1 tsp salt
2 tsp coriander seeds
2 tbsp lime juice
2 garlic cloves, crushed
1-in. piece ginger root, grated
1 clove
2 tsp garam masala
2 tsp chili powder
½ onion, chopped
1¼ cups natural yogurt
1 tbsp chopped fresh cilantro
lemon slices, to garnish
Cucumber Raita (page 234), to serve

1 Make 2–3 slashes with a sharp knife in the flesh of the chicken pieces.

2 Crush together the chilies, salt, coriander seeds, lime juice, garlic, ginger, and clove. Stir in the garam masala and chili powder. Transfer to a small saucepan and heat gently until aromatic.

3 Add the onion and fry. Then stir in the yogurt and remove the pan from the heat.

4 Arrange the chicken in a non-metallic dish and pour over the yogurt mixture. Cover and put in the refrigerator to marinate for 4 hours or overnight.

5 Arrange the chicken on a broiler tray and cook under a preheated very hot broiler or over a barbecue for 20–30 minutes, turning once, until the chicken juices run clear when the thickest parts of the portions are pierced with a sharp knife.

6 Sprinkle the chicken with chopped fresh cilantro. Serve hot or cold, garnished with the lemon slices, and accompanied by cucumber raita.

Step *2*

Step *3*

Step *4*

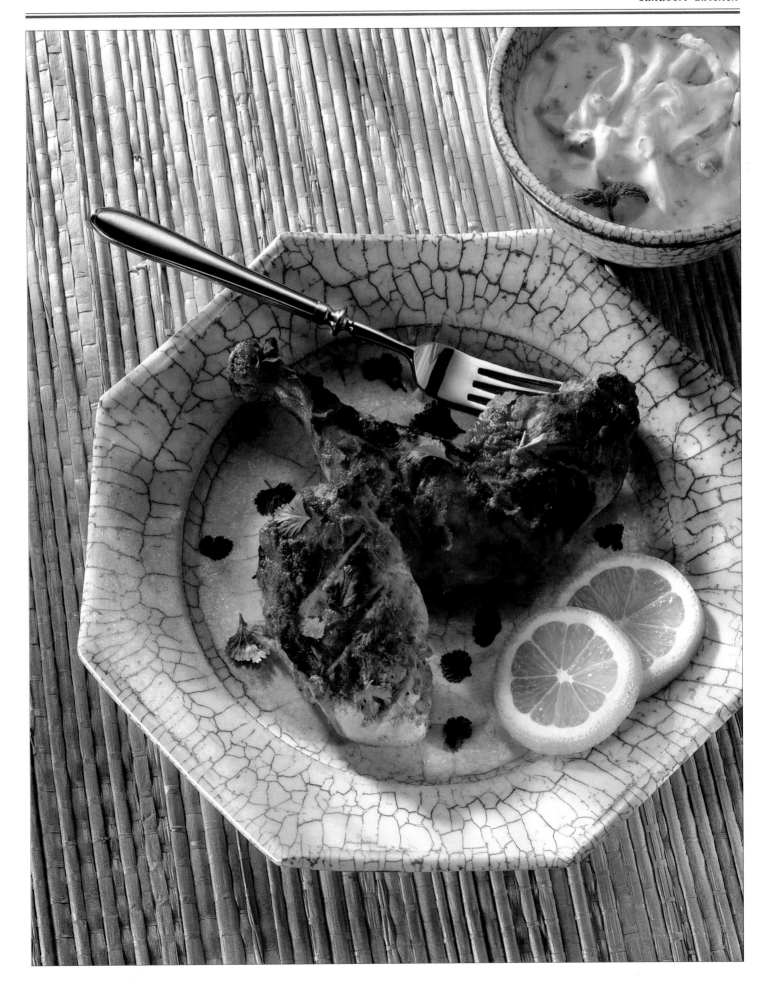

Chicken Jalfrezi

This is a quick and tasty way to use leftover roast chicken. The sauce can also be used for any cooked poultry, lamb, or beef.

SERVES 4

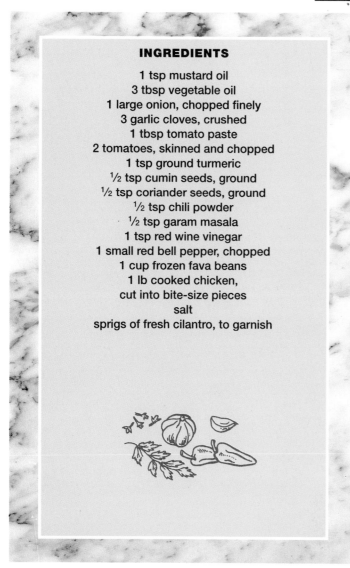

INGREDIENTS

1 tsp mustard oil
3 tbsp vegetable oil
1 large onion, chopped finely
3 garlic cloves, crushed
1 tbsp tomato paste
2 tomatoes, skinned and chopped
1 tsp ground turmeric
½ tsp cumin seeds, ground
½ tsp coriander seeds, ground
½ tsp chili powder
½ tsp garam masala
1 tsp red wine vinegar
1 small red bell pepper, chopped
1 cup frozen fava beans
1 lb cooked chicken,
cut into bite-size pieces
salt
sprigs of fresh cilantro, to garnish

1 Heat the mustard oil in a large skillet set over a high heat for about 1 minute until it begins to smoke. Add the vegetable oil, reduce the heat, and add the onion and the garlic. Fry the garlic and onion until they are golden.

2 Add the tomato paste, chopped tomatoes, turmeric, ground cumin and coriander seeds, chili powder, garam masala, and vinegar to the skillet. Stir the mixture until fragrant.

3 Add the red bell pepper and fava beans and stir for 2 minutes until the pepper is softened. Stir in the chicken and add salt to taste. Simmer gently for 6–8 minutes until the chicken is heated through and the beans are tender.

4 Serve garnished with sprigs of cilantro.

Step *1*

Step *2*

Step *3*

Chicken with Spicy Garbanzo Beans

This delicious combination of spiced garbanzo beans and chicken uses canned garbanzo beans which speeds up the cooking time considerably.

SERVES 4

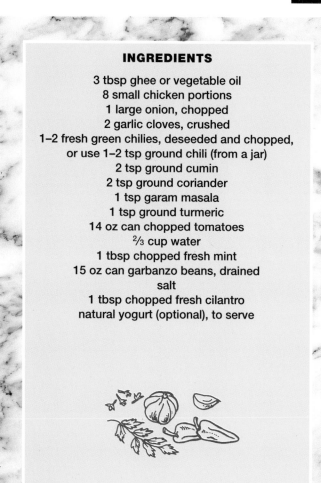

INGREDIENTS

3 tbsp ghee or vegetable oil
8 small chicken portions
1 large onion, chopped
2 garlic cloves, crushed
1–2 fresh green chilies, deseeded and chopped,
or use 1–2 tsp ground chili (from a jar)
2 tsp ground cumin
2 tsp ground coriander
1 tsp garam masala
1 tsp ground turmeric
14 oz can chopped tomatoes
⅔ cup water
1 tbsp chopped fresh mint
15 oz can garbanzo beans, drained
salt
1 tbsp chopped fresh cilantro
natural yogurt (optional), to serve

1 Heat the ghee or oil in a large saucepan and fry the chicken portions all over until sealed and lightly golden.

2 Remove from the pan. Add the onion, garlic, chili, and spices and cook very gently for 2 minutes, stirring frequently.

3 Stir in the tomatoes, water, mint, and garbanzo beans. Mix well, return the chicken portions to the pan, season with salt to taste, then cover, and simmer gently for about 20 minutes or until the chicken is tender and cooked through.

4 Taste and adjust the seasoning if necessary, then sprinkle with the chopped cilantro, and serve hot, drizzled with yogurt, if using.

Step *1*

Step *2*

Step *3*

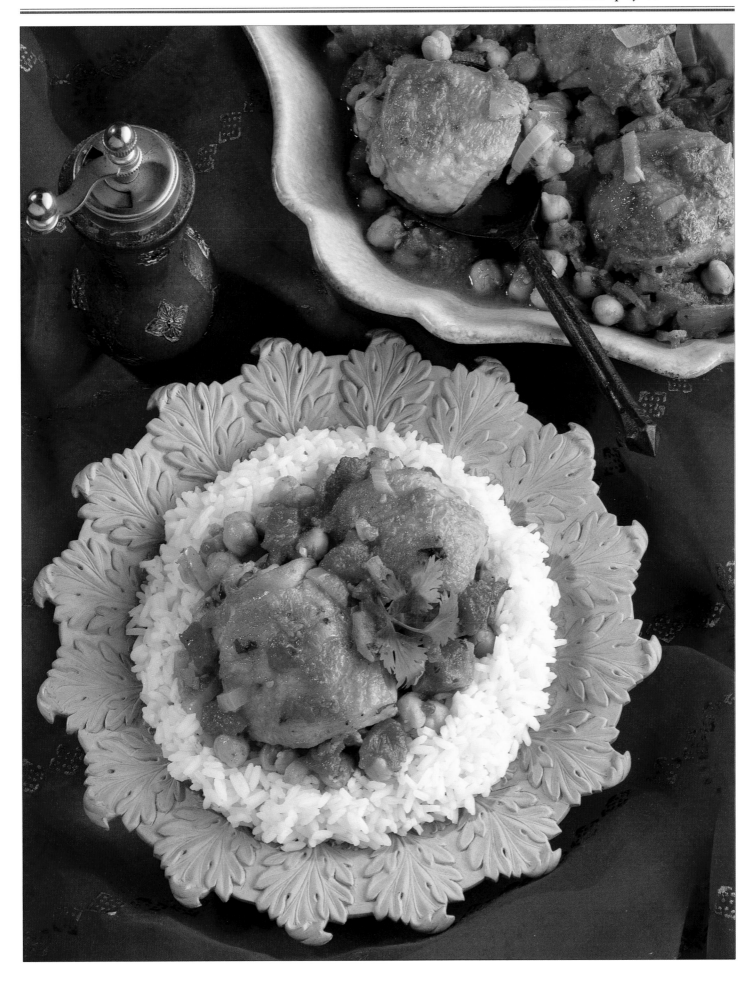

Chicken Tikka Masala

Serve this very rich dish with an array of accompaniments to provide a
balance and to neutralize the fiery flavors.

SERVES 4

INGREDIENTS

½ onion, chopped coarsely
3 tbsp tomato paste
1 tsp cumin seeds
1-in. piece ginger root, chopped
3 tbsp lemon juice
2 garlic cloves, crushed
2 tsp chili powder
1½ lb boneless chicken
salt and pepper
sprigs of mint, to garnish

MASALA SAUCE

2 tbsp ghee
1 onion, sliced
1 tbsp black onion seeds
3 garlic cloves, crushed
2 fresh green chilies, chopped
7 oz can tomatoes
½ cup natural yogurt
½ cup coconut milk
1 tbsp chopped fresh cilantro
1 tbsp chopped fresh mint
2 tbsp lemon or lime juice
½ tsp garam masala

1 Purée the onion, tomato paste, cumin, ginger, lemon juice, garlic, chili powder, and salt and pepper in a food processor or blender and then transfer to a bowl. Alternatively, grind the cumin with a pestle and mortar and transfer to a bowl. Finely chop the onion and ginger and stir into the bowl with the tomato paste, lemon juice, salt and pepper, garlic, and chili powder.

2 Cut the chicken into 1¼ in. cubes. Stir into the bowl and leave to marinate for 2 hours.

3 Make the masala sauce. Heat the ghee in a large saucepan, add the onion, and stir over a medium heat for 5 minutes. Add the onion seeds, garlic, and chilies and cook until fragrant.

4 Add the tomatoes, yogurt, and coconut milk, bring to a boil, then simmer for 20 minutes.

5 Meanwhile, divide the chicken evenly between 8 oiled skewers and cook under a preheated very hot broiler for 15 minutes, turning frequently. Remove the chicken from the skewers and add to the sauce. Stir in the fresh cilantro, mint, lemon or lime juice, and garam masala. Serve garnished with sprigs of mint.

Step *1*

Step *2*

Step *3*

Shahi Murg

Shahi Murg is a traditional curry cooked in yogurt by a slow-cooking method that is used to make many of the sauces in India.

SERVES 4

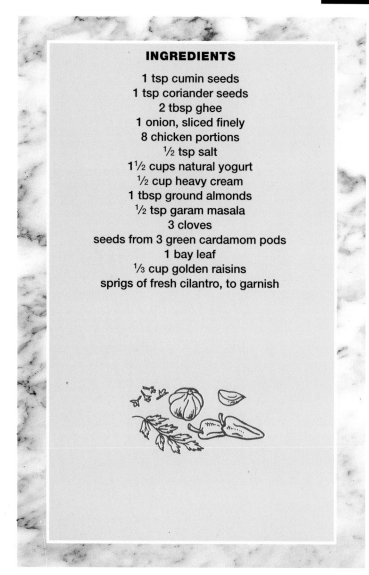

INGREDIENTS

1 tsp cumin seeds
1 tsp coriander seeds
2 tbsp ghee
1 onion, sliced finely
8 chicken portions
½ tsp salt
1½ cups natural yogurt
½ cup heavy cream
1 tbsp ground almonds
½ tsp garam masala
3 cloves
seeds from 3 green cardamom pods
1 bay leaf
⅓ cup golden raisins
sprigs of fresh cilantro, to garnish

1 Grind together the cumin and coriander seeds in a spice grinder or with a pestle and mortar.

2 Heat half the ghee in a large saucepan and cook the onion over a medium heat for 15 minutes, stirring occasionally, until the onion is very soft and sweet.

3 Meanwhile, heat the remaining ghee in a large skillet and brown the chicken portions well. Add the chicken to the onions.

4 Add the ground cumin and coriander, salt, yogurt, cream, almonds, and garam masala.

5 Bring to a gentle simmer, and add the cloves, cardamom, bay leaf, and golden raisins.

6 Simmer for 40 minutes until the chicken juices run clear when the thickest part of each piece is pierced with a sharp knife, and the sauce has reduced and thickened.

7 Serve garnished with sprigs of cilantro.

Step *1*

Step *3*

Step *4*

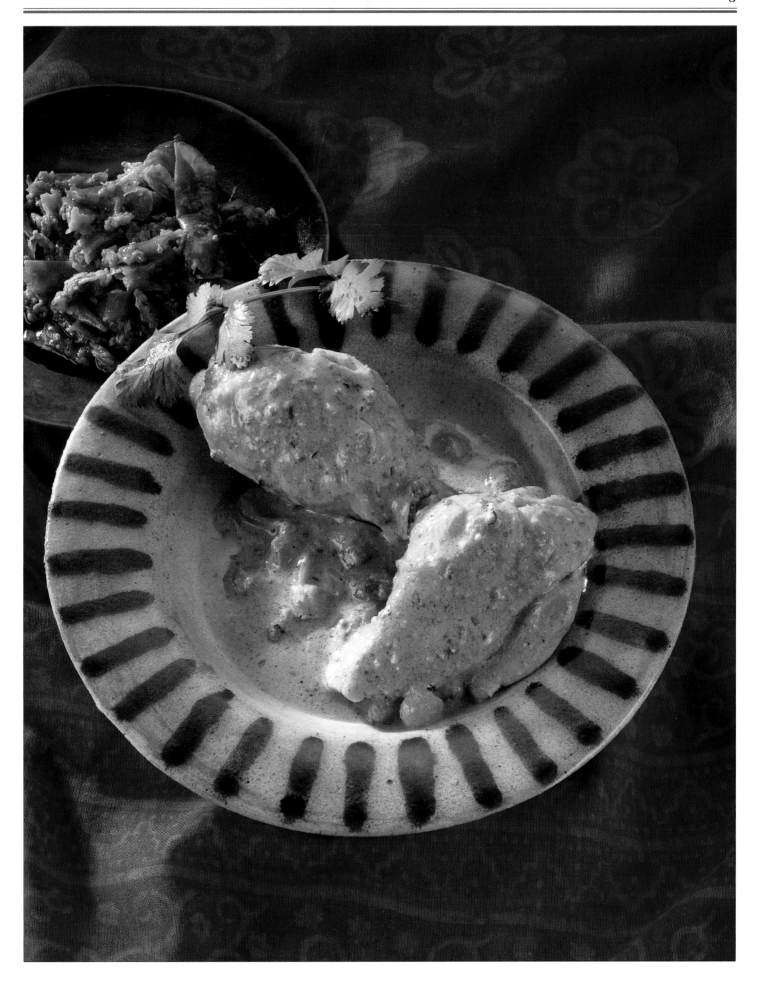

Stir-Fry Chicken Curry

A tasty mix of chicken, bell peppers, and cashew nuts is stir-fried with spices to give a delicious dish in minutes.

SERVES 4

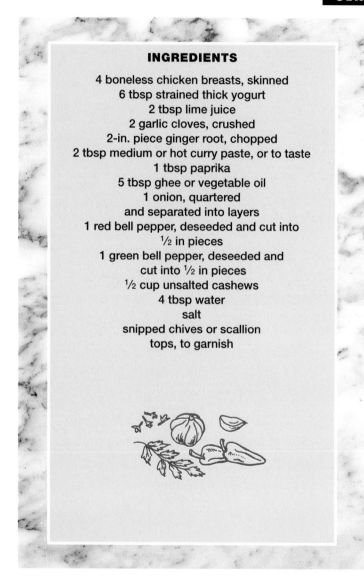

INGREDIENTS

4 boneless chicken breasts, skinned
6 tbsp strained thick yogurt
2 tbsp lime juice
2 garlic cloves, crushed
2-in. piece ginger root, chopped
2 tbsp medium or hot curry paste, or to taste
1 tbsp paprika
5 tbsp ghee or vegetable oil
1 onion, quartered
and separated into layers
1 red bell pepper, deseeded and cut into
½ in pieces
1 green bell pepper, deseeded and
cut into ½ in pieces
½ cup unsalted cashews
4 tbsp water
salt
snipped chives or scallion
tops, to garnish

1 Cut the chicken breasts into ½ in. wide strips and place in a bowl. Add the yogurt, lime juice, garlic, ginger, curry paste, and paprika. Season well and mix the ingredients together.

2 Heat the ghee or oil in a large skillet, add the onion, red and green bell peppers, and the cashews, and stir-fry over a moderate heat for 2 minutes. Remove from the skillet and reserve.

3 Stir the chicken mixture into the skillet and stir-fry for 4–5 minutes until well sealed and cooked though.

4 Add the water and mix well, then return the vegetables to the skillet, reduce the heat, and cook gently for 2 minutes. Serve at once, sprinkled with chives or scallion tops.

Step *1*

Step *3*

Step *4*

Chicken & Vegetable Rice

Boneless chicken breasts may be used here instead of the drumsticks, if preferred, in which case, slash them diagonally through the flesh.

SERVES 4-6

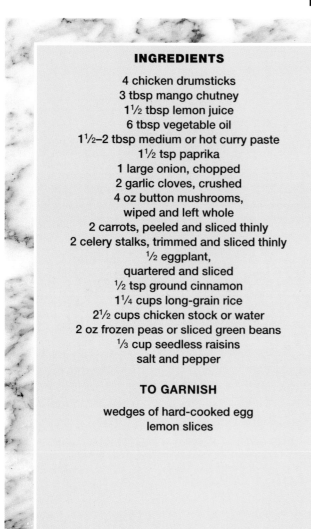

INGREDIENTS

4 chicken drumsticks
3 tbsp mango chutney
1½ tbsp lemon juice
6 tbsp vegetable oil
1½–2 tbsp medium or hot curry paste
1½ tsp paprika
1 large onion, chopped
2 garlic cloves, crushed
4 oz button mushrooms,
wiped and left whole
2 carrots, peeled and sliced thinly
2 celery stalks, trimmed and sliced thinly
½ eggplant,
quartered and sliced
½ tsp ground cinnamon
1¼ cups long-grain rice
2½ cups chicken stock or water
2 oz frozen peas or sliced green beans
⅓ cup seedless raisins
salt and pepper

TO GARNISH

wedges of hard-cooked egg
lemon slices

1 Slash the drumsticks twice on each side, cutting through the skin and deep into the flesh each time. Mix the chutney with the lemon juice, 1 tablespoon oil, the curry paste, and paprika. Brush over the drumsticks and reserve the remainder for later.

2 Heat 2 tablespoons of oil in a skillet and fry the drumsticks over a moderate heat for about 5 minutes until sealed and golden brown all over.

3 Meanwhile, heat the remaining oil in a saucepan, add the onion, mushrooms, carrots, celery, eggplant, garlic, and cinnamon, and fry lightly for 1 minute. Stir in the rice and cook gently for 1 minute, stirring until the rice is well coated with the oil. Add the stock and the remaining mango chutney mixture, peas, raisins, and salt and pepper to taste. Bring to a boil.

4 Reduce the heat and add the drumsticks to the mixture, pushing them down into the liquid. Cover and cook gently for 25 minutes until the liquid has been absorbed and the drumsticks are tender.

5 Remove the drumsticks from the pan and keep warm. Fluff up the rice mixture and transfer to a warm serving plate. Arrange the rice into a nicely shaped mound and place the drumsticks around it. Garnish the dish with wedges of hard-cooked egg and lemon.

Step *1*

Step *3*

Step *4*

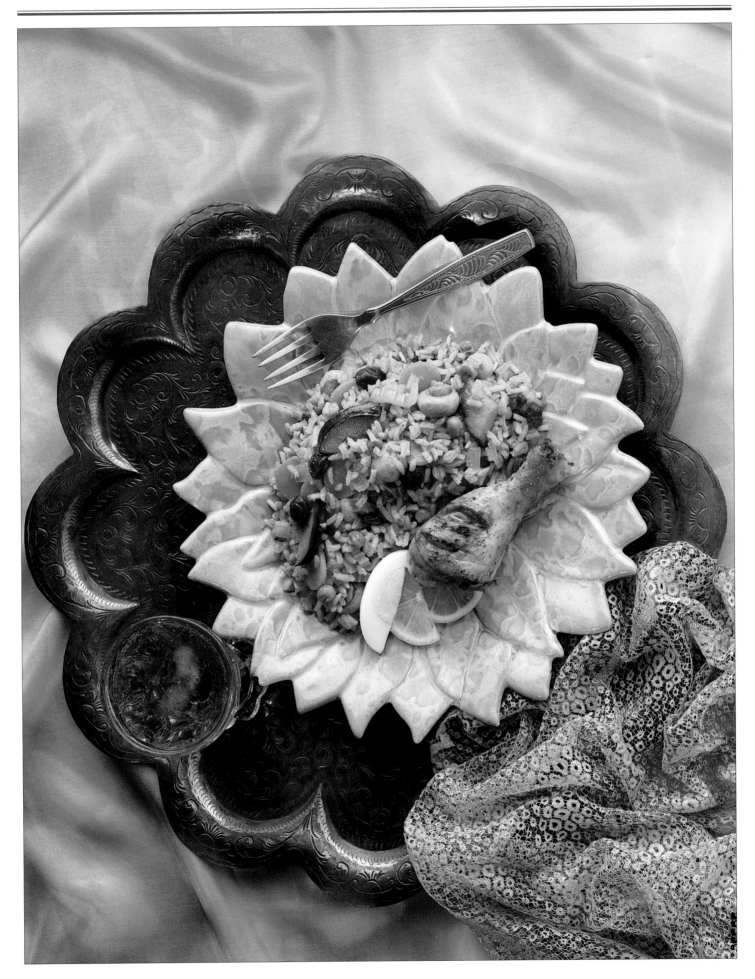

Balti Chicken Paneer

This recipe is based on one of the most popular Balti recipes, chicken in butter sauce. The poppy seeds in the sauce enhance the nutty taste of the almonds.

SERVES 4

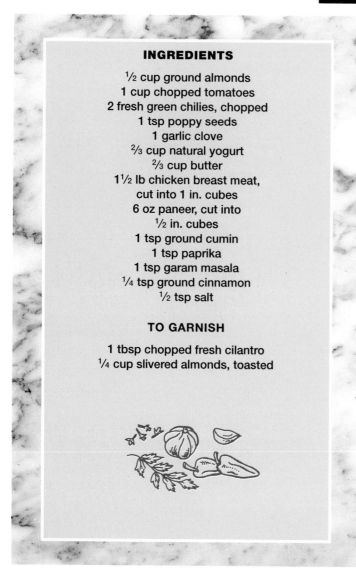

INGREDIENTS

½ cup ground almonds
1 cup chopped tomatoes
2 fresh green chilies, chopped
1 tsp poppy seeds
1 garlic clove
⅔ cup natural yogurt
⅔ cup butter
1½ lb chicken breast meat,
cut into 1 in. cubes
6 oz paneer, cut into
½ in. cubes
1 tsp ground cumin
1 tsp paprika
1 tsp garam masala
¼ tsp ground cinnamon
½ tsp salt

TO GARNISH

1 tbsp chopped fresh cilantro
¼ cup slivered almonds, toasted

1 Put the ground almonds, tomatoes, chilies, poppy seeds, and garlic in a food processor or blender and blend to a smooth paste. Alternatively, push the tomatoes through a strainer, finely chop the chilies and garlic, crush the poppy seeds, then mix together the tomatoes, chilies, garlic, poppy seeds, and ground almonds. Stir the yogurt into the tomato mixture.

2 Heat the butter in a karahi or wok, add the chicken, and stir-fry for 5 minutes.

3 Add the paneer, cumin, paprika, garam masala, cinnamon, and salt and stir-fry for 1 minute.

4 Add the tomato and yogurt mixture slowly to prevent the yogurt curdling. Simmer for 10–15 minutes until the chicken juices run clear when the chicken is pierced with a sharp knife.

5 Serve garnished with the cilantro and toasted slivered almonds.

Step *1*

Step *3*

Step *4*

Chicken in Spiced Coconut Cream

*This delicious combination would make a perfect dinner or supper party
main course – and what's more it is quick and simple to prepare.*

SERVES 4

INGREDIENTS

4 boneless chicken breasts, skinned
6 tbsp vegetable oil
2 onions, quartered and thinly sliced
1 garlic clove, crushed
1-in. piece ginger root, chopped finely
1–2 fresh green chilies, deseeded
and finely chopped,
or use 1–2 tsp ground chili (in a jar)
6 oz mushrooms, wiped and sliced
2 tsp medium curry powder
2 tsp ground coriander
½ tsp ground cinnamon
1 tbsp sesame seeds
⅔ cup chicken stock
7 oz can chopped tomatoes
1¼ cups coconut milk
salt
sprigs of cilantro, to garnish

1 Cut each chicken breast into 3 diagonal pieces. Heat 4 tablespoons of oil in a saucepan and fry the chicken pieces until lightly sealed all over. Remove from the pan and reserve.

2 Add the remaining oil to the pan and gently fry the onions, garlic, ginger, chilies, mushrooms, curry powder, spices, and sesame seeds for 3 minutes, stirring frequently.

3 Stir in the chicken stock, tomatoes, and coconut milk. Season with salt to taste and bring to a boil.

4 Reduce the heat, return the chicken pieces to the pan, and simmer gently, uncovered, for about 12 minutes, or until the chicken is tender and cooked through and the sauce has thickened, stirring occasionally. Garnish with sprigs of cilantro.

Step *2*

Step *3*

Step *4*

Saffron Chicken

This is a beautifully aromatic dish, the full fragrance of which brings to mind the opulent days of the maharajahs.

SERVES 4

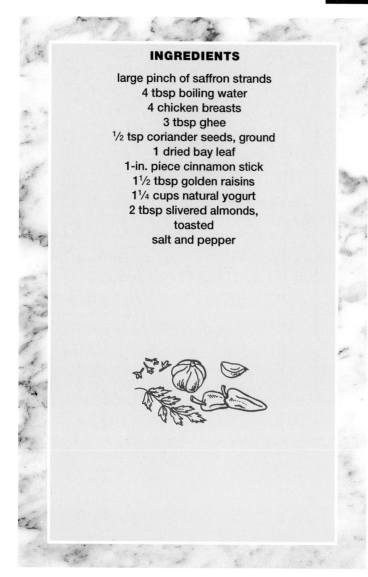

INGREDIENTS

large pinch of saffron strands
4 tbsp boiling water
4 chicken breasts
3 tbsp ghee
½ tsp coriander seeds, ground
1 dried bay leaf
1-in. piece cinnamon stick
1½ tbsp golden raisins
1¼ cups natural yogurt
2 tbsp slivered almonds,
toasted
salt and pepper

1 Combine the saffron with the boiling water, and leave to steep for 10 minutes.

2 Season the chicken breasts with salt and pepper.

3 Heat the ghee in a large skillet, add the chicken breasts, and brown on both sides. Cook in batches if necessary. Remove the chicken from the skillet.

4 Reduce the heat to medium and add the coriander to the skillet, stir once, then add the bay leaf, cinnamon stick, golden raisins, and the saffron with the soaking water, all at once.

5 Return the chicken to the skillet. Cover and simmer gently for 40–50 minutes or until the chicken juices run clear when the thickest part of each piece is pierced with a sharp knife. Remove the skillet from the heat and gently stir the yogurt into the sauce.

6 Discard the bay leaf and cinnamon stick. Scatter over the toasted almonds and serve.

Step *1*

Step *2*

Step *3*

Karahi Chicken

A karahi is an extremely versatile two-handled metal pan, similar to a wok. Food is always cooked over a high heat in a karahi.

SERVES 4–6

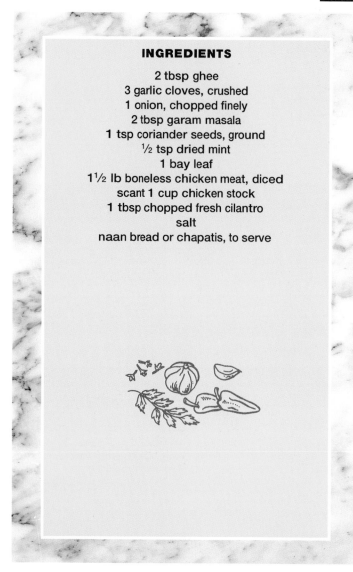

INGREDIENTS

2 tbsp ghee
3 garlic cloves, crushed
1 onion, chopped finely
2 tbsp garam masala
1 tsp coriander seeds, ground
½ tsp dried mint
1 bay leaf
1½ lb boneless chicken meat, diced
scant 1 cup chicken stock
1 tbsp chopped fresh cilantro
salt
naan bread or chapatis, to serve

1 Heat the ghee in a karahi, wok, or a large, heavy skillet and add the garlic and onion. Stir for about 4 minutes until the onion is golden.

2 Stir in the garam masala, ground coriander, mint, and bay leaf.

3 Add the chicken and cook over a high heat, stirring occasionally, for about 5 minutes.

4 Add the stock and simmer for 10 minutes, until the sauce has thickened and the chicken juices run clear when the meat is tested with a sharp knife.

5 Stir in the fresh cilantro, salt to taste, and serve immediately with naan bread or chapatis.

Step *1*

Step *3*

Step *4*

Chicken & Aromatic Almonds

*Rich and delicious – enjoy the succulence of chicken cooked with yogurt,
cream and ground almonds flavored with aromatic garam masala.*

SERVES 4

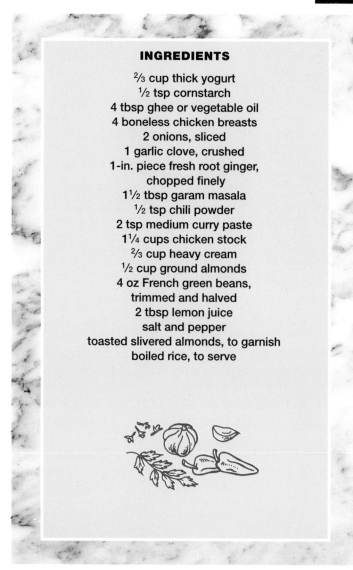

INGREDIENTS

⅔ cup thick yogurt
½ tsp cornstarch
4 tbsp ghee or vegetable oil
4 boneless chicken breasts
2 onions, sliced
1 garlic clove, crushed
1-in. piece fresh root ginger,
chopped finely
1½ tbsp garam masala
½ tsp chili powder
2 tsp medium curry paste
1¼ cups chicken stock
⅔ cup heavy cream
½ cup ground almonds
4 oz French green beans,
trimmed and halved
2 tbsp lemon juice
salt and pepper
toasted slivered almonds, to garnish
boiled rice, to serve

1 Smoothly blend the yogurt in a small bowl with the cornstarch. Heat the ghee or oil in a large flameproof casserole. Add the chicken breasts and fry until golden all over. Remove the chicken from the casserole and reserve.

2 Add the onions, garlic, and ginger to the casserole and fry gently for 3 minutes, then add the garam masala, chili powder, and curry paste, and fry gently for 1 minute. Stir in the stock, yogurt, and salt and pepper to taste and bring to a boil, stirring all the time.

3 Return the chicken breasts to the casserole, then cover, and simmer gently for 25 minutes. Remove the chicken to a dish and keep warm.

4 Blend the cream with the ground almonds and add to the sauce. Stir in the green beans and lemon juice and boil vigorously for 1 minute, stirring all the time.

5 Return the chicken to the casserole, cover, and cook gently for a further 10 minutes. Garnish with toasted slivered almonds and serve with rice.

Step *2*

Step *4*

Step *5*

MEAT DISHES

Curries are, of course, the most famous of Indian meat dishes, but they are by no means the only dishes the Indian culinary repertoire has to offer! Consider stir-fries with a blend of Indian spices, skewered kebabs of meat and vegetables, vegetables stuffed with savory meat and rice or lentil mixtures, risotto-style combinations of meat with rice, or meat roasted tandoori-style.

Even then there are differences and variations which give a typical national dish a distinctive regional flavor all of its own. South India curries, for example, are fierce and fiery, while North Kashmiri and Punjab meat dishes are comparatively mild and flavored with onion and garlic. Western or Goan dishes are slow-cooked, hot and thickened with coconut milk, whereas Eastern meat dishes rely upon spices such as mustard, cumin, and anise for their distinctive flavor and originality.

Meat dishes often incorporate vegetables to make a complete meal in one pan. This type of dish is ideal when cooking a quick evening meal, as you need to serve only naan bread or chapatis as an accompaniment: it also saves time spent washing dishes.

Masala Lamb & Lentils

This recipe makes a good warming winter curry.
Gram lentils have been used here but you could use split yellow peas.

SERVES 4

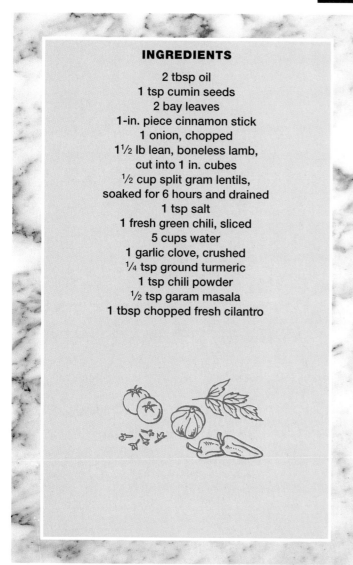

INGREDIENTS

2 tbsp oil
1 tsp cumin seeds
2 bay leaves
1-in. piece cinnamon stick
1 onion, chopped
1½ lb lean, boneless lamb,
cut into 1 in. cubes
½ cup split gram lentils,
soaked for 6 hours and drained
1 tsp salt
1 fresh green chili, sliced
5 cups water
1 garlic clove, crushed
¼ tsp ground turmeric
1 tsp chili powder
½ tsp garam masala
1 tbsp chopped fresh cilantro

1 Heat the oil in a karahi or wok and add the cumin seeds, bay leaves, and cinnamon, and fry until the seeds start popping.

2 Add the onion to the pan and stir-fry until golden brown.

3 Stir the lamb into the onion and stir-fry until browned.

4 Add the lentils, salt, chili, water, garlic, turmeric, and chili powder. Bring to a boil, then simmer for 1 hour until the meat and lentils are tender.

5 Taste and stir the garam masala into the pan, and cook for a further 5 minutes. Stir in the cilantro, and serve.

Step *1*

Step *3*

Step *4*

Lamb Tikka Masala

This is a very rich dish, and is best enjoyed with simple accompaniments, such as dal, naan bread, a salad, and some plain basmati rice.

SERVES 6

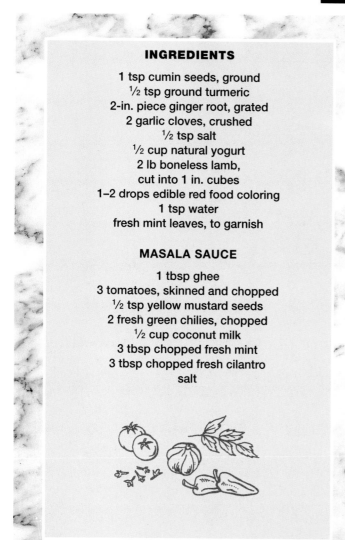

INGREDIENTS

1 tsp cumin seeds, ground
½ tsp ground turmeric
2-in. piece ginger root, grated
2 garlic cloves, crushed
½ tsp salt
½ cup natural yogurt
2 lb boneless lamb,
cut into 1 in. cubes
1–2 drops edible red food coloring
1 tsp water
fresh mint leaves, to garnish

MASALA SAUCE

1 tbsp ghee
3 tomatoes, skinned and chopped
½ tsp yellow mustard seeds
2 fresh green chilies, chopped
½ cup coconut milk
3 tbsp chopped fresh mint
3 tbsp chopped fresh cilantro
salt

1 Combine the cumin, turmeric, ginger, garlic, salt, and yogurt in a bowl. Stir in the lamb until evenly coated with the sauce. Dilute the food coloring with the water, and add to the bowl, stirring well. Marinate in the refrigerator for 2 hours. Soak 6 wooden skewers in warm water for 15 minutes.

2 Make the masala sauce. Heat the ghee in a large saucepan and add the tomatoes, mustard seeds, green chilies, and coconut milk. Bring to a boil, then simmer for 20 minutes until the tomatoes have broken down. Stir occasionally.

3 Thread the pieces of lamb onto 6 oiled skewers. Set on a broiler pan and cook under a preheated very hot broiler for 15–20 minutes, turning occasionally.

4 Stir the mint and fresh cilantro into the sauce, and season with salt.

5 Carefully remove the lamb from the skewers. Stir the lamb into the sauce and serve garnished with fresh mint leaves.

Step *1*

Step *3*

Step *5*

Lamb Pasanda

This dish is as close as one gets to the classic curry that springs to mind when Indian cooking is mentioned.

SERVES 4

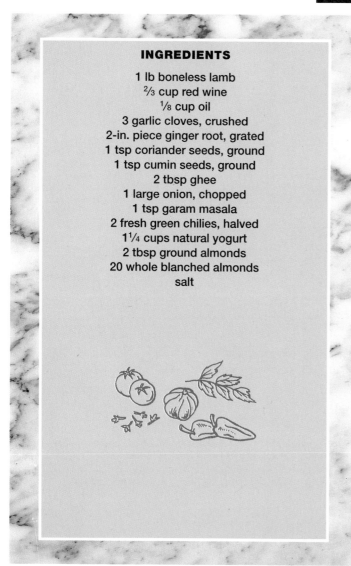

INGREDIENTS

1 lb boneless lamb
⅔ cup red wine
⅛ cup oil
3 garlic cloves, crushed
2-in. piece ginger root, grated
1 tsp coriander seeds, ground
1 tsp cumin seeds, ground
2 tbsp ghee
1 large onion, chopped
1 tsp garam masala
2 fresh green chilies, halved
1¼ cups natural yogurt
2 tbsp ground almonds
20 whole blanched almonds
salt

1 Cut the lamb into strips 1 in. across and 4 inches long. Set aside.

2 Combine the red wine, oil, garlic, ginger, ground coriander, and cumin seeds in a large non-metallic bowl. Stir in the lamb and leave to marinate for 1 hour.

3 Heat the ghee in a skillet and fry the onion until brown.

4 Drain the lamb, reserving the contents of the bowl. Pat the lamb dry with paper towels. Add the lamb to the skillet and stir over a high heat until it is evenly sealed and browned.

5 Add the contents of the bowl to the pan, and bring to a gentle boil. Add the garam masala, chilies, yogurt, ground almonds, whole almonds, and salt to taste. Cover and simmer for 12–15 minutes until the lamb is tender.

Step *3*

Step *4*

Step *5*

Lamb & Potato Masala

It's so easy to create delicious Indian dishes at home – simply open a can
of curry sauce and add a few interesting ingredients.

SERVES 4

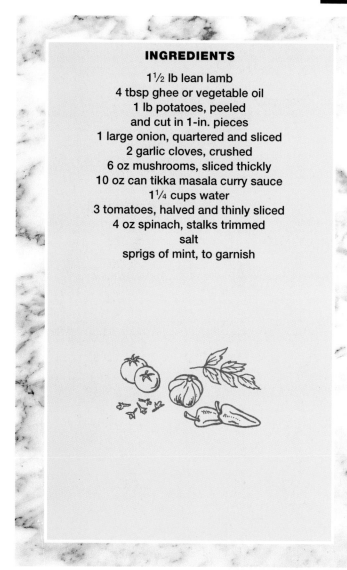

INGREDIENTS

1½ lb lean lamb
4 tbsp ghee or vegetable oil
1 lb potatoes, peeled
and cut in 1-in. pieces
1 large onion, quartered and sliced
2 garlic cloves, crushed
6 oz mushrooms, sliced thickly
10 oz can tikka masala curry sauce
1¼ cups water
3 tomatoes, halved and thinly sliced
4 oz spinach, stalks trimmed
salt
sprigs of mint, to garnish

1 Cut the lamb into 1 in. cubes. Heat the ghee or oil in a large pan, add the lamb, and fry over moderate heat for 3 minutes or until sealed all over. Remove from the pan.

2 Add the potatoes, onion, garlic, and mushrooms and fry for 3–4 minutes, stirring frequently. Stir the curry sauce and water into the pan, add the lamb, mix well, and season with salt to taste. Cover and cook very gently for 1 hour or until the lamb is tender and cooked through, stirring occasionally.

3 Add the tomatoes and spinach to the pan, pushing the leaves well down into the mixture. Cover and cook for a further 10 minutes until the spinach is tender. Garnish with sprigs of mint and serve hot.

Step *1*

Step *2*

Step *2*

Lamb Do Pyaza

Do Pyaza usually indicates a dish of meat cooked with plenty of onions,
and in this recipe the onions are cooked in two different ways.

SERVES 4

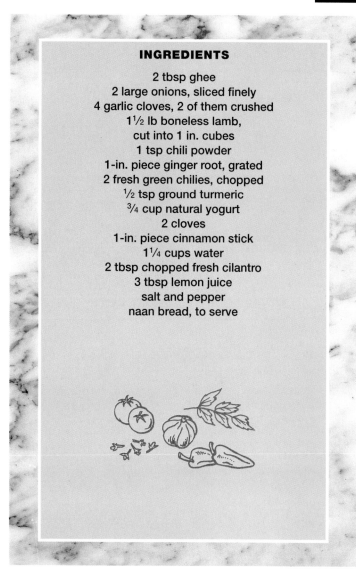

INGREDIENTS

2 tbsp ghee
2 large onions, sliced finely
4 garlic cloves, 2 of them crushed
1½ lb boneless lamb,
cut into 1 in. cubes
1 tsp chili powder
1-in. piece ginger root, grated
2 fresh green chilies, chopped
½ tsp ground turmeric
¾ cup natural yogurt
2 cloves
1-in. piece cinnamon stick
1¼ cups water
2 tbsp chopped fresh cilantro
3 tbsp lemon juice
salt and pepper
naan bread, to serve

1 Heat the ghee in a large saucepan and add 1 of the onions and all the garlic. Cook for 2–3 minutes, stirring constantly.

2 Add the lamb and brown all over. Remove and set aside.

3 Add the chili powder, ginger, chilies, and turmeric and stir for a further 30 seconds.

4 Add plenty of salt and pepper, the yogurt, cloves, cinnamon, and water. Return the lamb to the pan. Bring to a boil then simmer for 10 minutes.

5 Transfer to an ovenproof dish and cook uncovered in a preheated oven, 350°F, for 40 minutes. Check the seasoning.

6 Stir in the remaining onion and cook uncovered for a further 40 minutes.

7 Add the fresh cilantro and lemon juice. Serve with naan bread.

Step *1*

Step *3*

Step *6*

Rogan Josh

Rogan Josh is one of the best-known curries and is a great favorite in restaurants. The title means 'red curry', the red being provided by the chilies.

SERVES 6

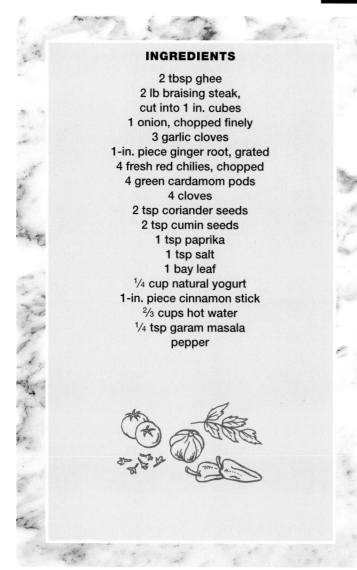

INGREDIENTS

2 tbsp ghee
2 lb braising steak,
cut into 1 in. cubes
1 onion, chopped finely
3 garlic cloves
1-in. piece ginger root, grated
4 fresh red chilies, chopped
4 green cardamom pods
4 cloves
2 tsp coriander seeds
2 tsp cumin seeds
1 tsp paprika
1 tsp salt
1 bay leaf
¼ cup natural yogurt
1-in. piece cinnamon stick
⅔ cups hot water
¼ tsp garam masala
pepper

1 Heat the ghee in a large flameproof casserole and brown the meat in batches. Set aside in a bowl.

2 Add the onion to the ghee and stir over a high heat for 3–4 minutes.

3 Grind together the garlic, ginger, chilies, cardamom, cloves, coriander, cumin, paprika, and salt.

4 Add the spice paste and bay leaf to the casserole and stir until fragrant.

5 Return the meat and any juices in the bowl to the casserole and simmer for 2–3 minutes.

6 Gradually stir the yogurt into the casserole keeping the sauce simmering.

7 Stir in the cinnamon and hot water, and pepper to taste.

8 Cover the casserole and cook in a preheated oven, 350°F, for 1¼ hours, stirring frequently, until the meat is very tender and the sauce is slightly reduced.

9 Discard the cinnamon stick and stir in the garam masala. Remove surplus oil from the surface of the casserole before serving.

Step *2*

Step *4*

Step *7*

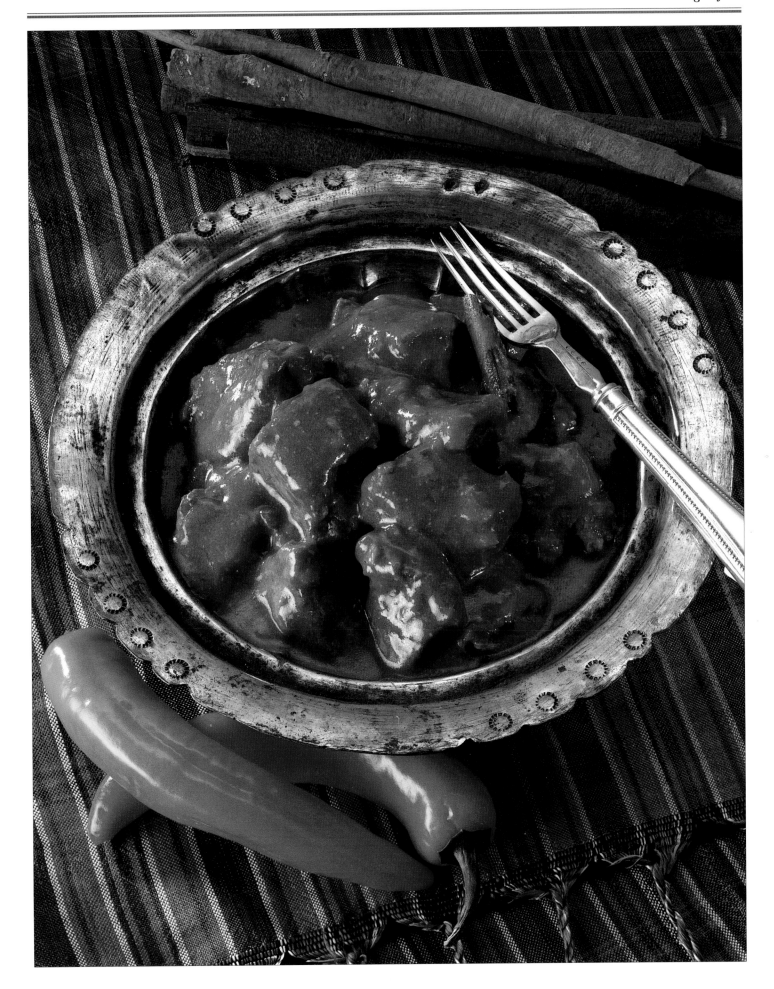

Lamb Phall

Do try to use freshly ground whole spices for this delicious hot curry, as they will make the overall taste more complex and enjoyable.

SERVES 4–6

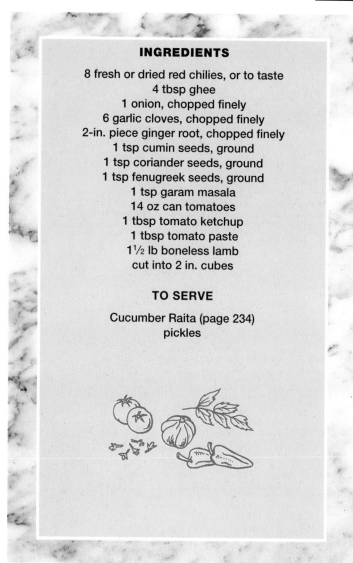

INGREDIENTS

8 fresh or dried red chilies, or to taste
4 tbsp ghee
1 onion, chopped finely
6 garlic cloves, chopped finely
2-in. piece ginger root, chopped finely
1 tsp cumin seeds, ground
1 tsp coriander seeds, ground
1 tsp fenugreek seeds, ground
1 tsp garam masala
14 oz can tomatoes
1 tbsp tomato ketchup
1 tbsp tomato paste
1½ lb boneless lamb
cut into 2 in. cubes

TO SERVE

Cucumber Raita (page 234)
pickles

1 Chop 4 of the chilies and leave the other 4 whole.

2 Heat half of the ghee in a saucepan and add the onion, garlic, and ginger. Stir over a medium heat until golden.

3 Stir the cumin, coriander, fenugreek, and garam masala into the onion mixture. Cook over a medium heat for 10 minutes.

4 Stir the canned tomatoes, tomato ketchup, tomato paste, and the whole and chopped chilies into the pan, and bring to a gentle boil. Cook over a low heat for 10 minutes.

5 Meanwhile, heat the remaining ghee in a flameproof casserole and cook the meat until evenly sealed. Cook in batches if necessary.

6 Transfer the sauce to the casserole with the meat, cover and cook in a preheated oven, 350°F, for 1½ hours until the meat is tender.

7 Serve with cucumber raita and pickles.

Step *2*

Step *3*

Step *4*

Lamb Bhuna

The pungent flavors of the chilies in this curry should not hide the flavors of the other spices.

SERVES 4–6

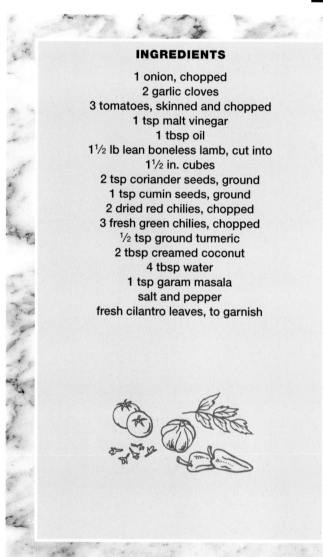

INGREDIENTS

1 onion, chopped
2 garlic cloves
3 tomatoes, skinned and chopped
1 tsp malt vinegar
1 tbsp oil
1½ lb lean boneless lamb, cut into
1½ in. cubes
2 tsp coriander seeds, ground
1 tsp cumin seeds, ground
2 dried red chilies, chopped
3 fresh green chilies, chopped
½ tsp ground turmeric
2 tbsp creamed coconut
4 tbsp water
1 tsp garam masala
salt and pepper
fresh cilantro leaves, to garnish

1 Purée the onion, garlic, tomatoes, and vinegar in a food processor or blender. Alternatively, chop the vegetables finely by hand, then mix with the vinegar. Set aside.

2 Heat the oil in a large skillet and brown the meat for 5–10 minutes. Remove and set aside.

3 Reduce the heat and add the ground coriander seeds, cumin, chilies, and turmeric to the skillet. Stir continuously until the spices are fragrant.

4 Increase the heat again and add the onion mixture. Stir-fry for 5 minutes until nearly dry.

5 Return the meat to the skillet. Combine the coconut and water and add to the skillet. Simmer for 45–60 minutes until the meat is tender. Stir in the garam masala and season to taste.

6 Serve garnished with fresh cilantro leaves.

Step *1*

Step *3*

Step *5*

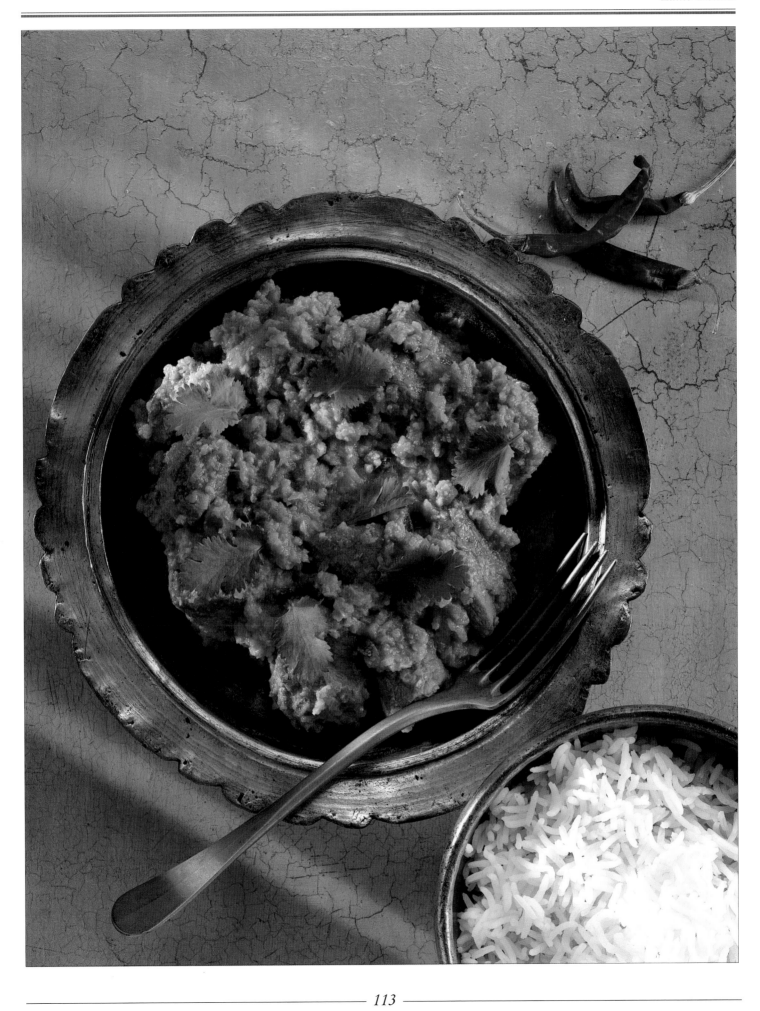

Spicy Beef & Yogurt

Deliciously quick and easy – stir-fried steak is served with a tangy eggplant yogurt dressing. Use mild, medium, or hot curry paste according to taste.

SERVES 4

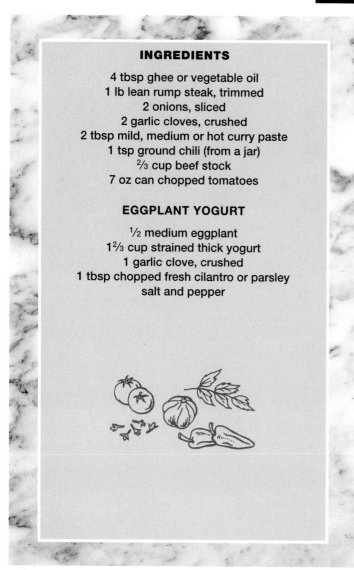

INGREDIENTS

4 tbsp ghee or vegetable oil
1 lb lean rump steak, trimmed
2 onions, sliced
2 garlic cloves, crushed
2 tbsp mild, medium or hot curry paste
1 tsp ground chili (from a jar)
²⁄₃ cup beef stock
7 oz can chopped tomatoes

EGGPLANT YOGURT

½ medium eggplant
1²⁄₃ cup strained thick yogurt
1 garlic clove, crushed
1 tbsp chopped fresh cilantro or parsley
salt and pepper

1 First make the eggplant yogurt. Peel the eggplant and cut into 1 in. pieces. Place in the top half of a steamer and steam over boiling water for 10 minutes.

2 Meanwhile, whip the yogurt with the garlic, cilantro, and salt and pepper to taste. Allow the cooked eggplant to cool slightly, then mash with a fork. Stir the eggplant into the yogurt.

3 Heat the ghee or oil in a large skillet, add the beef and onions, and stir-fry for 5 minutes until the beef is sealed all over.

4 Stir in the garlic, curry paste, chili, stock, and tomatoes and bring to a boil. Cover, reduce the heat, and simmer gently for 5 minutes, stirring occasionally. Serve hot with the eggplant yogurt.

Step *1*

Step *3*

Step *4*

Beef & Mushroom Curry

Vary the meat here according to personal taste, using lean lamb or pork (leg or shoulder cuts are ideal) instead of beef. Omit the finishing touches (see step 4) if wished.

SERVES 4

INGREDIENTS

1½ lb lean braising beef, trimmed
3 tbsp vegetable oil
2 onions, sliced
2 garlic cloves, crushed
1-in. piece ginger root,
chopped finely
2 fresh green chilies, deseeded and chopped,
or use 1–2 tsp ground chili (from a jar)
1½ tbsp medium curry paste
1 tsp ground coriander
6–8 oz mushrooms, sliced thickly
3½ cups stock
3 tomatoes, chopped
½–1 tsp salt
2 oz creamed coconut, chopped
2 tbsp ground almonds

TO FINISH

2 tbsp vegetable oil
1 green or red bell pepper,
deseeded and cut into thin strips
6 scallions, trimmed and sliced
1 tsp cumin seeds

1 Cut the beef into small bite-size cubes. Heat the oil in a saucepan, add the beef, and fry until sealed, stirring frequently. Remove from the pan.

2 Add the onions, garlic, ginger, chilies, curry paste, and coriander to the pan and cook gently for 2 minutes. Stir in the mushrooms, stock, and tomatoes, and season with salt to taste. Return the beef to the pan, then cover and simmer very gently for 1¼–1½ hours or until the beef is tender.

3 Stir the chopped creamed coconut and ground almonds into the curry, then cover the pan, and cook gently for 3 minutes.

4 Meanwhile, heat the remaining oil in a skillet, add the bell pepper strips and scallion slices, and fry gently until glistening and tender-crisp. Stir in the cumin seeds and fry gently for 30 seconds, then spoon the mixture over the curry, and serve at once.

Step *2*

Step *3*

Step *4*

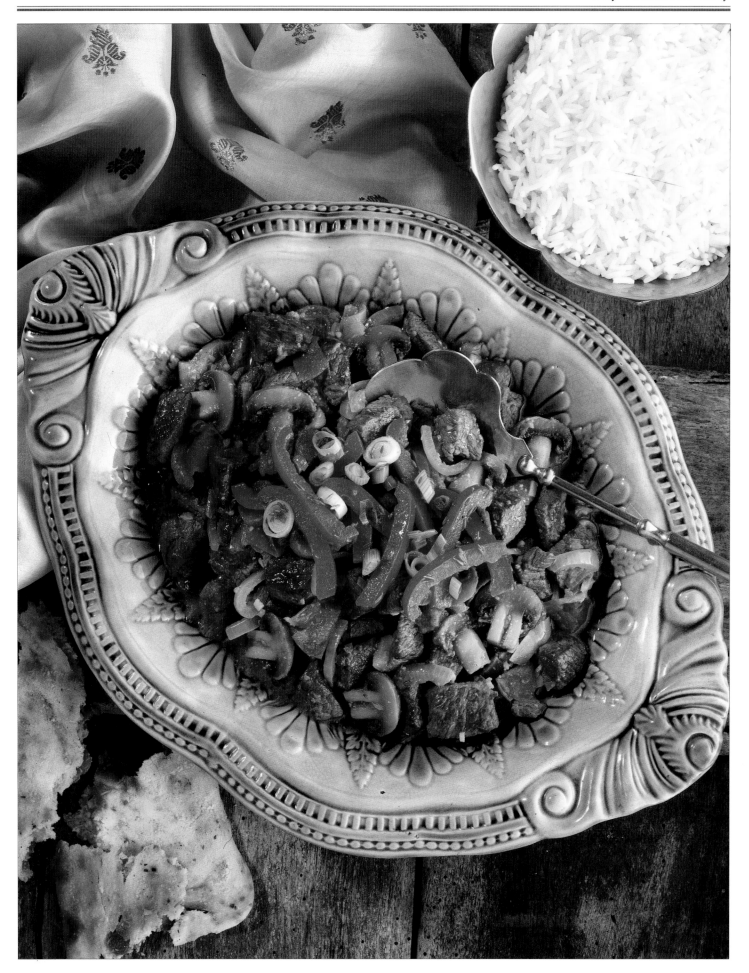

Vindaloo Curry

*Vindaloo is the classic fiery curry that originates in Goa. The 'vin' in the
title refers to the vinegar that is added to tenderize the meat.*

SERVES 4–6

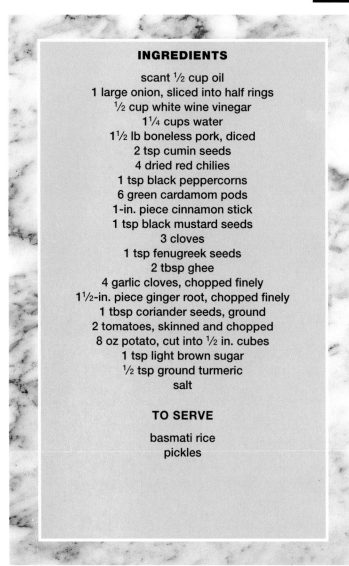

INGREDIENTS

scant ½ cup oil
1 large onion, sliced into half rings
½ cup white wine vinegar
1¼ cups water
1½ lb boneless pork, diced
2 tsp cumin seeds
4 dried red chilies
1 tsp black peppercorns
6 green cardamom pods
1-in. piece cinnamon stick
1 tsp black mustard seeds
3 cloves
1 tsp fenugreek seeds
2 tbsp ghee
4 garlic cloves, chopped finely
1½-in. piece ginger root, chopped finely
1 tbsp coriander seeds, ground
2 tomatoes, skinned and chopped
8 oz potato, cut into ½ in. cubes
1 tsp light brown sugar
½ tsp ground turmeric
salt

TO SERVE

basmati rice
pickles

1 Heat the oil in a large saucepan and fry the onion until golden brown. Set aside.

2 Combine 2 tablespoons of the vinegar with 1 tablespoon of the water in a large bowl. Add the pork and stir together well. Set aside.

3 In a food processor or blender mix the onions, cumin, chilies, peppercorns, cardamom, cinnamon, mustard seeds, cloves, and fenugreek to a paste. Alternatively, grind the ingredients together with a pestle and mortar. Transfer to a bowl and add the remaining vinegar.

4 Heat the ghee in a skillet or casserole and cook the pork until it is browned on all sides.

5 Add the garlic, ginger, and ground coriander and stir until fragrant, then add the tomatoes, potato, brown sugar, turmeric, and remaining water. Add salt to taste and bring to a boil. Stir in the spice paste, cover, reduce the heat, and simmer for 1 hour until the pork is tender.

6 Serve with basmati rice and pickles.

Step 2

Step 3

Step 5

Pork Chops & Spicy Red Beans

A tasty and substantial dish that is packed full of goodness. The spicy bean mixture,
served on its own, also makes a good accompaniment to meat or chicken dishes.

SERVES 4

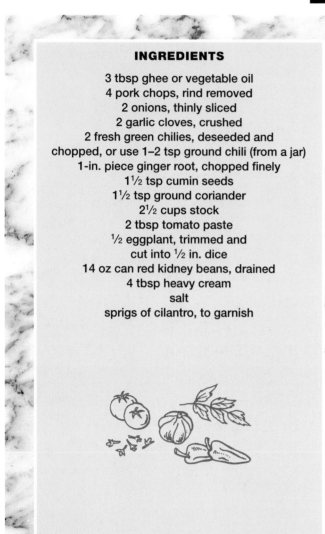

INGREDIENTS

3 tbsp ghee or vegetable oil
4 pork chops, rind removed
2 onions, thinly sliced
2 garlic cloves, crushed
2 fresh green chilies, deseeded and
chopped, or use 1–2 tsp ground chili (from a jar)
1-in. piece ginger root, chopped finely
1½ tsp cumin seeds
1½ tsp ground coriander
2½ cups stock
2 tbsp tomato paste
½ eggplant, trimmed and
cut into ½ in. dice
14 oz can red kidney beans, drained
4 tbsp heavy cream
salt
sprigs of cilantro, to garnish

1 Heat the ghee or oil in a large skillet, add the pork chops, and fry until sealed and browned on both sides. Remove from the skillet and reserve.

2 Add the sliced onions, garlic, chilies, ginger, and spices and fry gently for 2 minutes. Stir in the stock, tomato paste, eggplant, and salt to taste.

3 Bring the mixture to a boil, place the chops on top, then cover, and simmer gently over medium heat for 30 minutes, or until the chops are tender and cooked through.

4 Remove the chops for a moment and stir the red kidney beans and cream into the mixture. Return the chops to the skillet, cover, and heat through gently for 5 minutes. Taste and adjust the seasoning, if necessary. Serve hot, garnished with sprigs of cilantro.

Step *1*

Step *3*

Step *4*

VEGETABLE DISHES

By applying myriad methods born of a centuries-old tradition of vegetarianism, Indian cooks turn the simplest vegetables into the most extraordinary feasts. Many of these cooking methods are completely alien to us, but they result in dishes which are both a joy to eat and nourishing to the mind and body.

Indian vegetarianism is due mainly to the predominant Hindu religion, with its reverence for animals – especially cows – and its ideal of harmonizing the diet with the need of the soul. A vegetarian diet is followed also because vegetable cropping is a more efficient use of land than keeping animals for food. Although we may be used to eating vegetables with Indian meals in restaurants, restaurant cuisine differs markedly from native cuisine. In India, vegetables are relied on to play a leading role in a meal – in a bhaji (a dry curry) for example, or puréed in a bhartha.

Vegetable curries are flavored simply, and the spices and sauces can be easily transferred between vegetables. For example, the sauce Palak Paneer (page 160) can be used with other leafy vegetables, and your own spice mixes experimented with when you have some vegetables to cook.

Vegetable Curry

This colorful and interesting mixture of vegetables, cooked in a spicy sauce, is excellent served with pilau rice and naan bread.

SERVES 4

INGREDIENTS

8 oz turnips or rutabaga, peeled
1 eggplant, leaf end trimmed
12 oz new potatoes, scrubbed
8 oz cauliflower
8 oz button mushrooms, wiped
1 large onion
8 oz carrots, peeled
6 tbsp vegetable ghee or oil
2 garlic cloves, crushed
2-in. piece ginger root, chopped finely
1–2 fresh green chilies, deseeded and chopped
1 tbsp paprika
2 tsp ground coriander
1 tbsp mild or medium curry powder or paste
1¾ cups vegetable stock
14 oz can chopped tomatoes
1 green bell pepper, deseeded and sliced
1 tbsp cornstarch
⅔ cup coconut milk
2–3 tbsp ground almonds
salt
sprigs of cilantro, to garnish

1 Cut the turnips or rutabaga, eggplant, and potatoes into ½ in. cubes. Divide the cauliflower into small flowerets. Leave the mushrooms whole, or slice thickly, if preferred. Slice the onion and carrots.

2 Heat the ghee or oil in a large saucepan, add the onion, turnip or rutabaga, potato, and cauliflower, and cook slowly for 3 minutes, stirring frequently. Add the garlic, ginger, chili, and spices and cook for 1 minute, stirring frequently.

3 Add the stock, tomatoes, eggplant, and mushrooms and season with salt. Cover and simmer gently for about 30 minutes or until tender, stirring occasionally. Add the green bell pepper, cover, and continue cooking for a further 5 minutes.

4 Smoothly blend the cornstarch with the coconut milk and stir into the mixture. Add the ground almonds and simmer for 2 minutes, stirring all the time. Taste and adjust the seasoning, if necessary. Serve hot, garnished with sprigs of cilantro.

Step *1*

Step *2*

Step *3*

Mixed Vegetable Bhaji

In this delicious dish, the vegetables are first parboiled and then lightly braised with onions, tomatoes, and spices.

SERVES 4–6

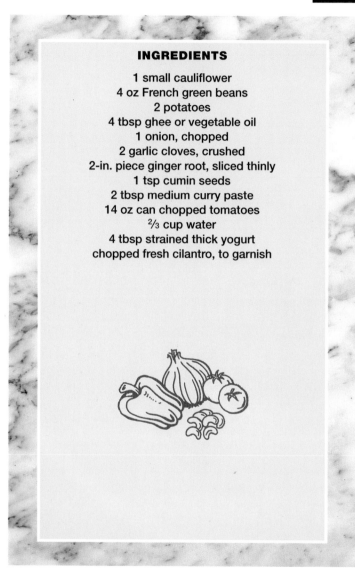

INGREDIENTS

1 small cauliflower
4 oz French green beans
2 potatoes
4 tbsp ghee or vegetable oil
1 onion, chopped
2 garlic cloves, crushed
2-in. piece ginger root, sliced thinly
1 tsp cumin seeds
2 tbsp medium curry paste
14 oz can chopped tomatoes
⅔ cup water
4 tbsp strained thick yogurt
chopped fresh cilantro, to garnish

1 Break the cauliflower into neat flowerets. Top, tail, and halve the beans. Peel and quarter the potatoes lengthwise, then cut each quarter into 3 pieces. Cook all the prepared vegetables in a pan of boiling, salted water for 5 minutes. Drain the vegetables well, return to the pan, and shake dry over a low heat for a few moments.

2 Heat the ghee or oil in a large skillet, add the onion, garlic, ginger, and cumin seeds, and stir-fry gently for 3 minutes. Stir in the curry paste, tomatoes, and water and bring to a boil. Reduce the heat and simmer the spicy mixture for 2 minutes.

3 Stir in the parboiled vegetables and mix lightly. Cover and cook gently for 5–8 minutes until just tender and cooked through. Whip the yogurt to soften, and drizzle the vegetable mixture with the yogurt. Sprinkle with the chopped cilantro. Serve hot.

Step *1*

Step *2*

Step *3*

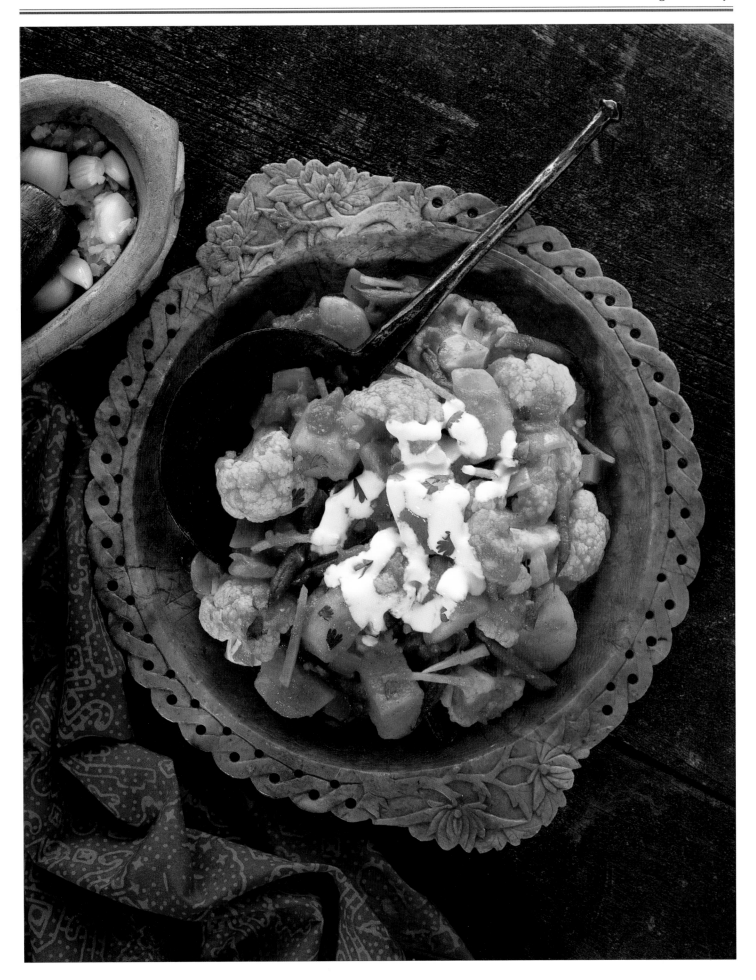

Brindil Bhaji

This is one of the most delicious of the bhaji dishes, and has a wonderful sweet spicy flavor.

SERVES 4

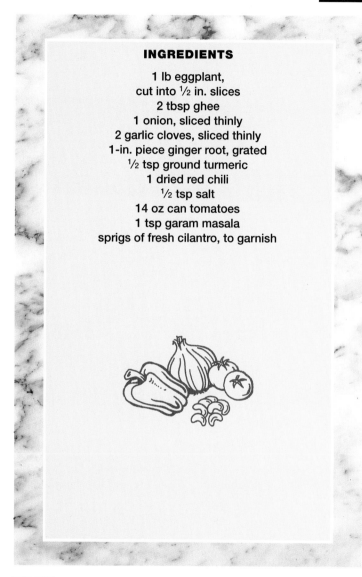

INGREDIENTS

1 lb eggplant,
cut into ½ in. slices
2 tbsp ghee
1 onion, sliced thinly
2 garlic cloves, sliced thinly
1-in. piece ginger root, grated
½ tsp ground turmeric
1 dried red chili
½ tsp salt
14 oz can tomatoes
1 tsp garam masala
sprigs of fresh cilantro, to garnish

1 Cut the eggplant slices into finger-width strips using a sharp knife.

2 Heat the ghee in a saucepan and cook the onion over a medium heat for 7–8 minutes, stirring constantly, until very soft.

3 Add the garlic and eggplant, increase the heat, and cook for 2 minutes.

4 Stir in the ginger, turmeric, chili, salt, and the tomatoes. Use the back of a wooden spoon to break up the tomatoes. Simmer uncovered for 15–20 minutes until the eggplant is very soft.

5 Stir in the garam masala. Simmer for a further 4–5 minutes.

6 Serve garnished with sprigs of fresh cilantro.

Step *1*

Step *2*

Step *4*

Roasted Eggplant Curry

*This is a rich vegetable dish, ideal served with a tandoori chicken and
naan bread. Also delicious as a vegetarian dish with rice.*

SERVES 6

INGREDIENTS

2 eggplants
1 cup natural yogurt
2 cardamom pods
½ tsp ground turmeric
1 dried red chili
½ tsp coriander seeds
½ tsp pepper
1 tsp garam masala
1 clove
2 tbsp sunflower oil
1 onion, sliced lengthwise
2 garlic cloves, crushed
1 tbsp grated ginger root
6 ripe tomatoes, peeled,
deseeded, and quartered
fresh cilantro, to garnish

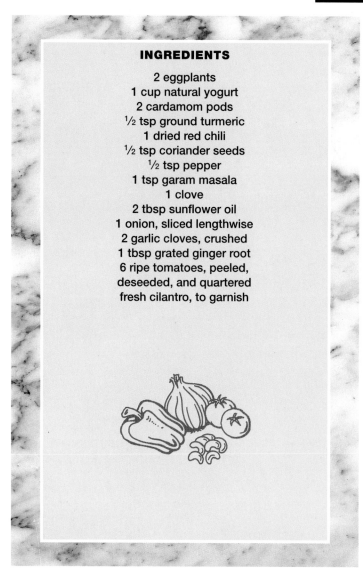

1 Roast the eggplants in a very hot oven for 15 minutes, turning once, or over a naked flame, turning frequently, until charred and black all over. This should take about 5 minutes. Peel under cold running water. Cut off the stem end and discard.

2 Put the peeled eggplants into a large bowl and mash lightly with a fork. Stir in the yogurt. Set aside.

3 Grind together the cardamom pods, turmeric, red chili, coriander seeds, pepper, garam masala, and clove with a large pestle and mortar or spice grinder.

4 Heat the oil in a wok or heavy skillet over a moderate heat and cook the onion, garlic, and ginger root until soft. Add the tomatoes and ground spices, and stir well.

5 Add the eggplant mixture to the pan and stir well. Cook for 5 minutes over a gentle heat, stirring constantly, until all the flavors are combined, and some of the liquid has evaporated. Serve immediately, garnished with cilantro.

Step *2*

Step *3*

Step *4*

Eggplant in Saffron Sauce

*Here is a quick and simple, delicately spiced and delicious way
to cook eggplant.*

SERVES 4

INGREDIENTS

a good pinch of saffron strands, crushed
1 tbsp boiling water
1 large eggplant
3 tbsp vegetable oil
1 large onion, coarsely chopped
2 garlic cloves, crushed
1-in. piece ginger root, chopped
1½ tbsp mild or medium curry paste
1 tsp cumin seeds
⅔ cup heavy cream
⅔ cup strained thick yogurt
2 tbsp mango chutney, chopped if necessary
salt and pepper

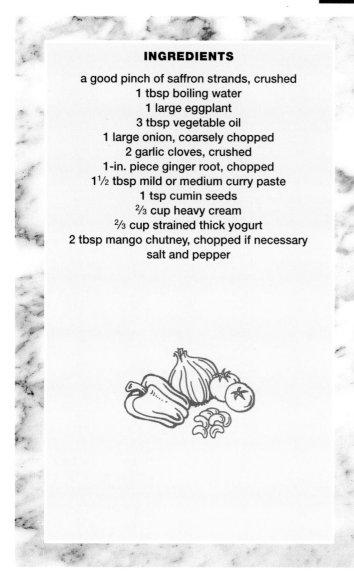

1 Place the saffron in a small bowl, add the boiling water, and leave to infuse for 5 minutes.

2 Trim the leaf end off the eggplant, cut lengthwise into fourths, then into ½ in. thick slices.

3 Heat the oil in a large skillet, add the onion, and cook gently for 3 minutes. Stir in the eggplant, garlic, ginger, curry paste, and cumin, and cook gently for 3 minutes.

4 Stir in the saffron infusion, cream, yogurt, and chutney, and cook gently for 8–10 minutes, stirring frequently, until the eggplant is cooked through and tender. Season with salt and pepper to taste and serve hot.

Step *2*

Step *3*

Step *4*

Eggplant Bhaji

To make the panch poran spice mix, combine 2 tsp cumin seeds, 2 tsp mustard seeds, 2 tsp fennel seeds, ¾ tsp fenugreek, and 1 tsp onion seeds.

SERVES 4

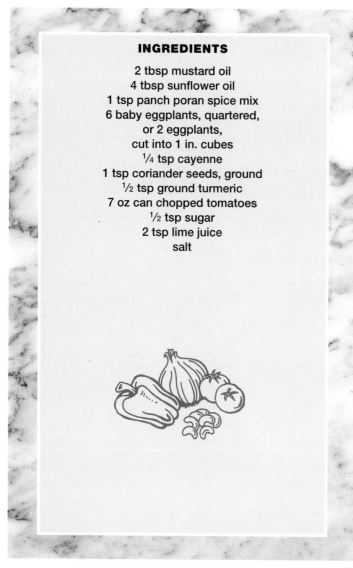

INGREDIENTS

2 tbsp mustard oil
4 tbsp sunflower oil
1 tsp panch poran spice mix
6 baby eggplants, quartered,
or 2 eggplants,
cut into 1 in. cubes
¼ tsp cayenne
1 tsp coriander seeds, ground
½ tsp ground turmeric
7 oz can chopped tomatoes
½ tsp sugar
2 tsp lime juice
salt

1 Heat the mustard oil in a wok or large skillet until it just starts to smoke. Reduce the heat and add the sunflower oil. Add the panch poran mix, stir once, and add the eggplant.

2 Add the cayenne, coriander, and turmeric, and stir over a high heat for 2–3 minutes until the eggplant is sealed on all sides.

3 Add the chopped tomatoes and their juice to the skillet and bring to a boil.

4 Simmer for 15 minutes or until the bhaji is nearly dry. Stir once or twice. Remove from the heat and stir in the sugar, the lime juice, and a pinch of salt.

5 Transfer to a warm serving dish, and serve immediately.

Step *1*

Step *3*

Step *4*

Long Beans with Tomatoes

Many Indian meals need some green vegetables to complement the
spicy dishes and to set off the rich sauces.

SERVES 4–6

INGREDIENTS

1 lb green beans, cut into
2-in. lengths
2 tbsp ghee
1-in. piece ginger root, grated
1 garlic clove, crushed
1 tsp ground turmeric
½ tsp cayenne
1 tsp ground coriander
4 tomatoes, skinned, deseeded, and diced
⅔ cup vegetable stock

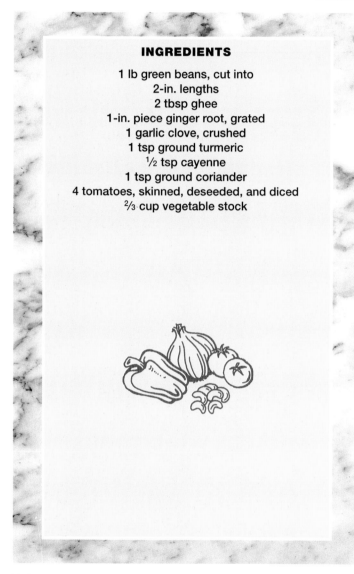

1 Blanch the beans quickly in boiling water, drain, and refresh under cold running water.

2 Melt the ghee in a large saucepan. Add the grated ginger root and crushed garlic, stir, and add the turmeric, cayenne, and coriander. Stir until fragrant, about 1 minute.

3 Add the tomatoes, tossing them until they are thoroughly coated in the spice mix.

4 Add the vegetable stock to the pan, bring to a boil, and cook over a medium-high heat for 10 minutes, until the sauce has thickened, stirring occasionally.

5 Add the beans, reduce the heat to moderate, and heat through for 5 minutes, stirring.

6 Transfer to a serving dish and serve immediately.

Step *1*

Step *3*

Step *4*

Okra Bhaji

*This is a very mild-tasting, rich curry, which would be an ideal
accompaniment to a tomato-based main-course curry.*

SERVES 4

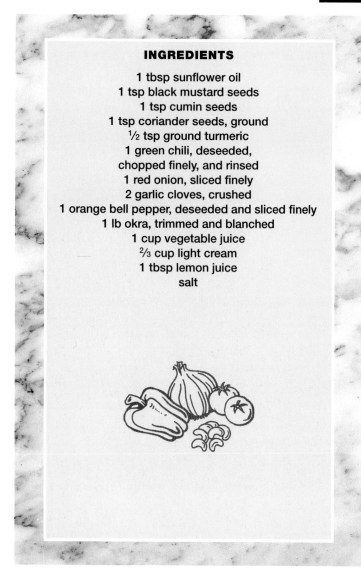

INGREDIENTS

1 tbsp sunflower oil
1 tsp black mustard seeds
1 tsp cumin seeds
1 tsp coriander seeds, ground
½ tsp ground turmeric
1 green chili, deseeded,
chopped finely, and rinsed
1 red onion, sliced finely
2 garlic cloves, crushed
1 orange bell pepper, deseeded and sliced finely
1 lb okra, trimmed and blanched
1 cup vegetable juice
⅔ cup light cream
1 tbsp lemon juice
salt

1 Heat the oil in a wok or large skillet. Add the mustard seeds and cover the pan until they start to pop. Stir in the cumin seeds, coriander, turmeric, and chili. Stir until fragrant, about 1 minute.

2 Add the onion, garlic, and bell pepper, and cook until soft, about 5 minutes, stirring frequently.

3 Add the okra to the pan and combine all the ingredients thoroughly.

4 Pour in the vegetable juice, bring to a boil, and cook over a high heat for 5 minutes, stirring occasionally.

5 When most of the liquid has evaporated, check the seasoning.

6 Add the cream, bring to a boil again, and continue to cook the mixture over a high heat for about 12 minutes until almost dry.

7 Sprinkle over the lemon juice and serve immediately.

Step *3*

Step *4*

Step *6*

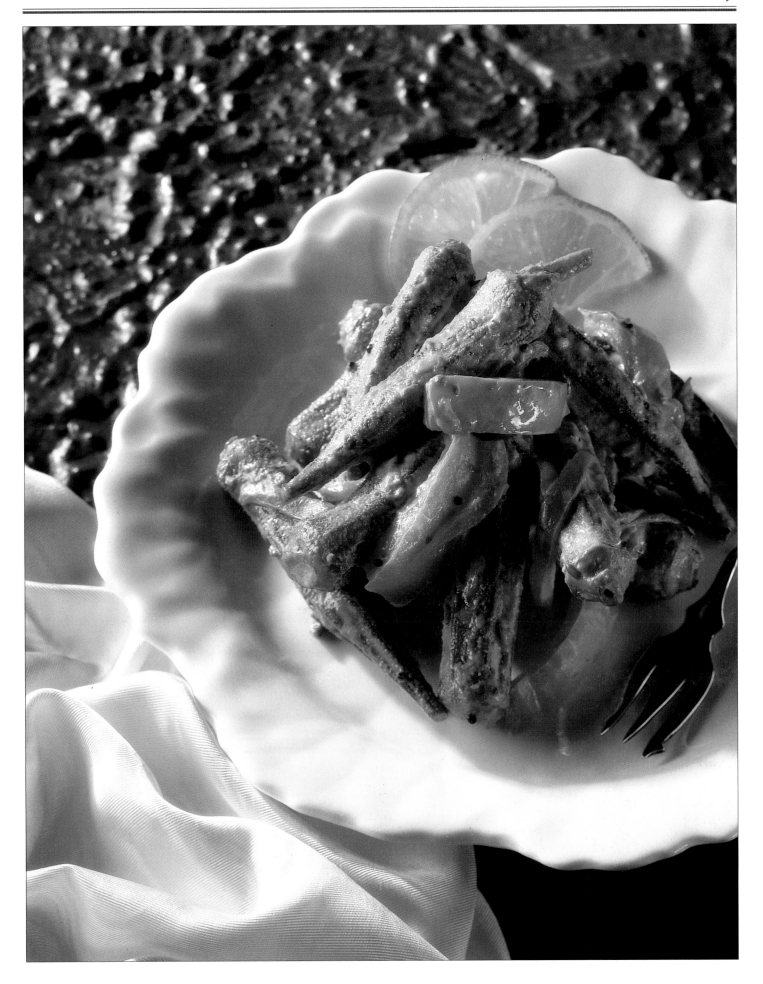

Curried Okra

Okra, also known as bhindi, ladies' fingers, and gumbo, are a favorite Indian vegetable.

SERVES 4

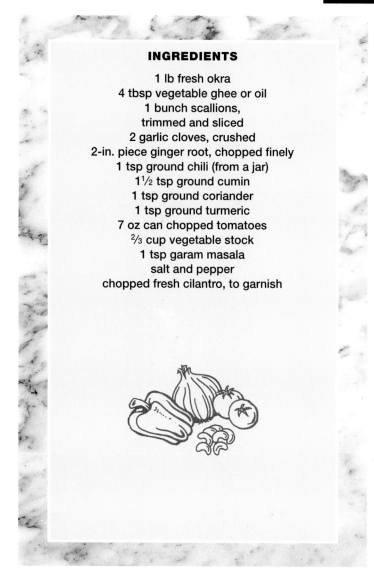

INGREDIENTS

1 lb fresh okra
4 tbsp vegetable ghee or oil
1 bunch scallions,
trimmed and sliced
2 garlic cloves, crushed
2-in. piece ginger root, chopped finely
1 tsp ground chili (from a jar)
1½ tsp ground cumin
1 tsp ground coriander
1 tsp ground turmeric
7 oz can chopped tomatoes
⅔ cup vegetable stock
1 tsp garam masala
salt and pepper
chopped fresh cilantro, to garnish

1 Wash the okra, trim off the stalks, and pat dry. Heat the ghee or oil in a large skillet, add the scallions, garlic, ginger, and chili, and fry gently for 1 minute, stirring frequently.

2 Stir in the spices and fry gently for 30 seconds, then add the tomatoes, stock, and okra. Season with salt and pepper to taste and simmer for about 15 minutes, stirring and turning the mixture occasionally. The okra should be cooked but still a little crisp.

3 Sprinkle with the garam masala, taste, and adjust the seasoning, if necessary. Garnish with the chopped cilantro and serve hot.

Step *1*

Step *2*

Step *3*

Spicy Cauliflower

This is a perfectly delicious way to serve cauliflower. It is a dry dish so can be enjoyed as a salad or at a picnic, or as an accompaniment to a dhansak or korma.

SERVES 4

INGREDIENTS

1 lb cauliflower, cut into flowerets
1 tbsp sunflower oil
1 garlic clove
½ tsp ground turmeric
1 tsp cumin seeds, ground
1 tsp coriander seeds, ground
1 tsp yellow mustard seeds
12 scallions, sliced finely
salt and pepper

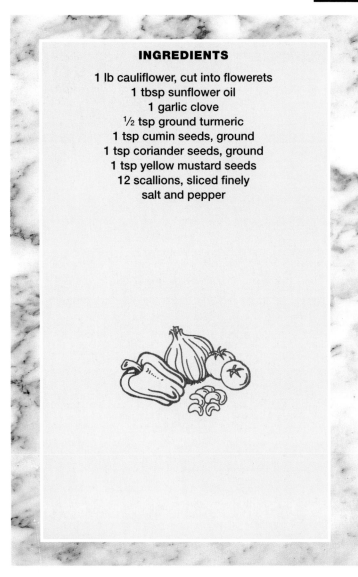

1 Blanch the cauliflower in boiling water, drain, and set aside. Cauliflower holds a lot of water, which tends to make it over-soft, so turn the flowerets upside-down at this stage and you will end up with a crisper result.

2 Heat the oil gently in a large, heavy skillet or wok. Add the garlic clove, turmeric, cumin, coriander, and mustard seeds. Stir well and cover the skillet.

3 When you hear the mustard seeds popping, add the scallions, and stir. Cook for 2 minutes, stirring constantly, to soften them a little. Season to taste.

4 Add the cauliflower and stir for 3–4 minutes until coated completely with the spices and thoroughly heated.

5 Remove the garlic clove and serve immediately.

Step *1*

Step *2*

Step *4*

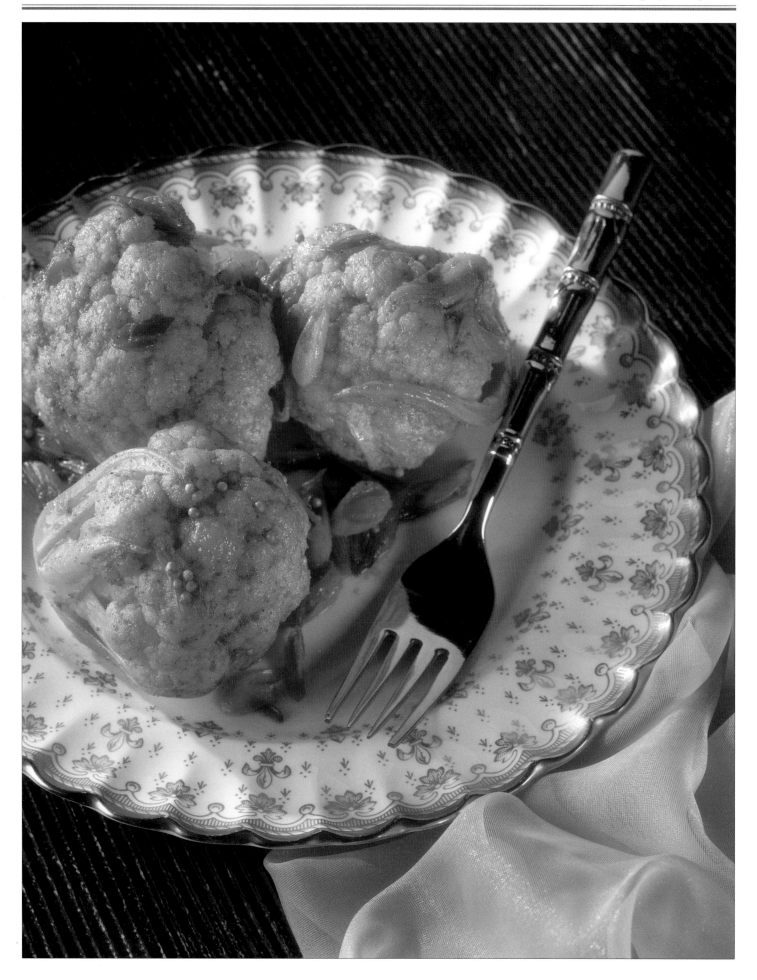

Spinach & Cauliflower Bhaji

This excellent vegetable dish goes well with most Indian food –
and it is simple and quick-cooking, too.

SERVES 4

INGREDIENTS

1 cauliflower
1 lb fresh spinach
4 tbsp vegetable ghee or oil
2 large onions, coarsely chopped
2 garlic cloves, crushed
1-in. piece ginger root, chopped finely
1¼ tsp cayenne, or to taste
1 tsp ground cumin
1 tsp ground turmeric
2 tsp ground coriander
14 oz can chopped tomatoes
1¼ cups vegetable stock
salt and pepper

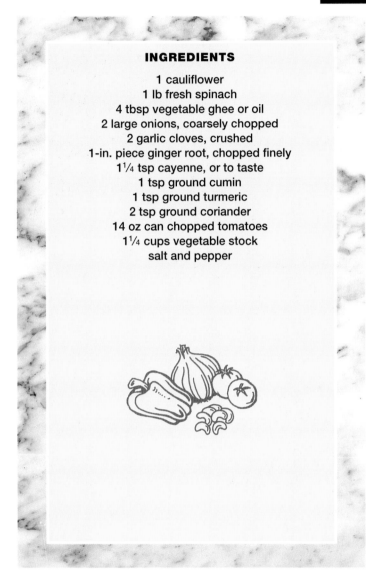

1 Divide the cauliflower into small flowerets, discarding the hard central stalk. Trim the stalks from spinach leaves. Heat the ghee or oil in a large saucepan, add the onions and cauliflower flowerets, and fry the vegetables gently for about 3 minutes, stirring frequently.

2 Add the garlic, ginger, and spices and cook gently for 1 minute. Stir in the tomatoes and the stock, and season with salt and pepper. Bring to a boil, cover, reduce the heat, and simmer gently for 8 minutes.

3 Add the spinach to the pan, stirring and turning to wilt the leaves. Cover and simmer gently for about 8–10 minutes, stirring frequently until the spinach has wilted and the cauliflower is tender. Serve hot.

Step *1*

Step *2*

Step *3*

Kashmiri Spinach

*This is an imaginative way to serve spinach, which adds a little zing to it.
It is a very simple dish, which will complement almost any curry.*

SERVES 4

INGREDIENTS

1lb spinach (or Swiss chard
or baby leaf spinach)
2 tbsp mustard oil
¼ tsp garam masala
1 tsp yellow mustard seeds
2 scallions, sliced

1 Remove the tough stalks from the spinach.

2 Heat the mustard oil in a wok or large heavy skillet until it smokes. Add the garam masala and mustard seeds. Cover the pan quickly – you will hear the mustard seeds popping inside.

3 When the popping has ceased, remove the cover, add the scallions, and stir in the spinach until wilted.

4 Continue cooking the spinach, uncovered, over a medium heat for 10–15 minutes, until most of the water has evaporated. Frozen spinach will not need so much cooking – cook it until most of the water has evaporated.

5 Remove the spinach and scallions with a perforated spoon in order to drain off any remaining liquid. This dish is more pleasant to eat when it is served as dry as possible. Serve immediately while it is piping hot.

Step *1*

Step *3*

Step *5*

Spicy Indian-Style Potatoes

Potatoes cooked this way are so delicious, yet quick and simple to prepare.
Cut the potatoes into similar-size pieces to make sure they cook evenly.

SERVES 4

INGREDIENTS

1½ lb potatoes
¼ cup ghee or butter
2 tbsp vegetable oil
1 tsp ground turmeric
1 large onion, quartered and sliced
2–3 garlic cloves, crushed
2-in. piece ginger root, chopped finely
1½ tsp cumin seeds
¼–½ tsp cayenne
2 tsp lemon juice
1 tbsp shredded mint leaves
salt
sprigs of mint, to garnish

1 Peel the potatoes and cut into ¾–1 in. cubes. Cook in a pan of boiling, salted water for 6–8 minutes or until knife-tip tender (do not overcook). Drain well, return to the pan, and shake dry over a moderate heat for a few moments.

2 Heat the ghee or butter and oil in a large skillet over medium heat. Stir in the turmeric, then add the onion and the potatoes, and fry for 4–5 minutes or until the mixture is beginning to brown, stirring and turning the vegetables frequently.

3 Stir in the garlic, ginger, cumin seeds, cayenne, and salt to taste. Fry over gentle heat for 1 minute, stirring all the time.

4 Transfer the potatoes to a warm serving dish. Add the lemon juice to the juices in the skillet, and spoon the mixture over the potatoes. Sprinkle with the shredded mint leaves, garnish with sprigs of mint, and serve hot.

Step *1*

Step *2*

Step *3*

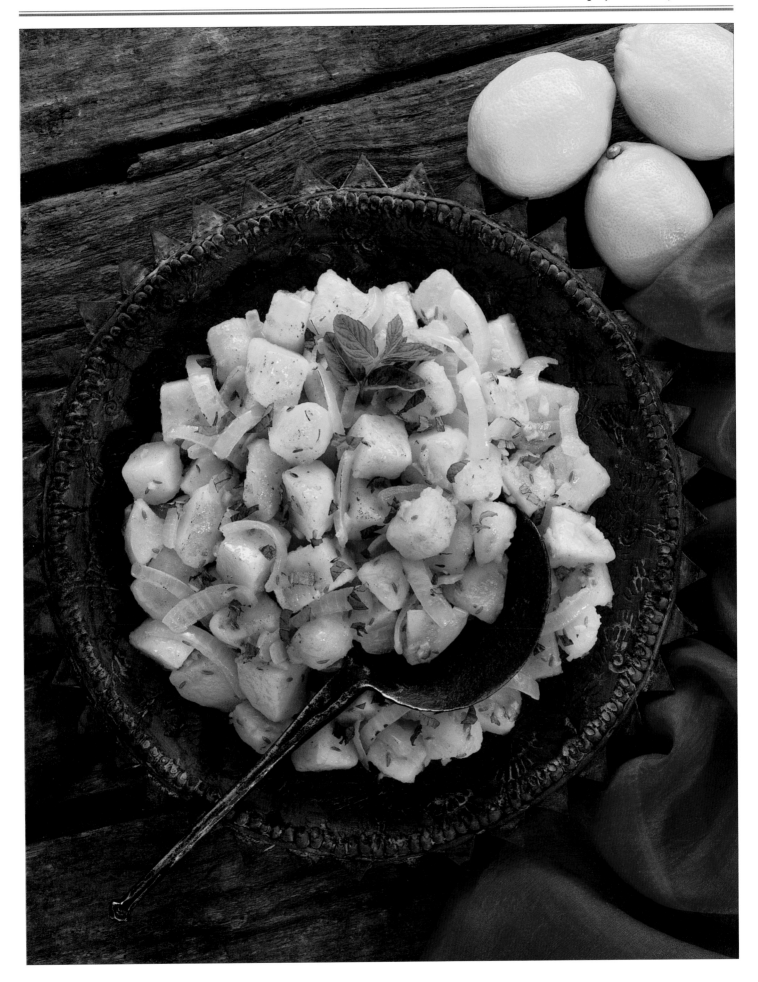

Fried Spiced Potatoes

Deliciously good and a super accompaniment to almost any main course dish, although rather high in calories!

SERVES 4–6

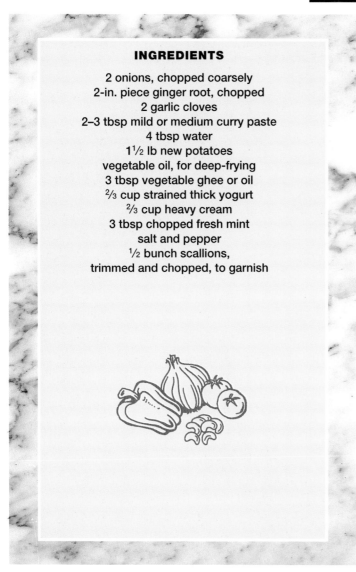

INGREDIENTS

2 onions, chopped coarsely
2-in. piece ginger root, chopped
2 garlic cloves
2–3 tbsp mild or medium curry paste
4 tbsp water
1½ lb new potatoes
vegetable oil, for deep-frying
3 tbsp vegetable ghee or oil
⅔ cup strained thick yogurt
⅔ cup heavy cream
3 tbsp chopped fresh mint
salt and pepper
½ bunch scallions,
trimmed and chopped, to garnish

1 Place the onions, ginger, garlic, curry paste, and water in a blender or food processor and process until smooth, scraping down the sides of the machine and blending again, if necessary.

2 Cut the potatoes into fourths – the pieces need to be about 1 in. in size – and pat dry with paper towels. Heat the oil in a deep-fat fryer to 350°F and fry the potatoes, in batches, for about 5 minutes or until golden brown, turning frequently. Remove from the fryer and drain on paper towels.

3 Heat the ghee or oil in a large skillet, add the onion mixture, and fry gently for 2 minutes, stirring all the time. Add the yogurt, cream, and 2 tablespoons of the mint and mix well.

4 Add the fried potatoes and stir until coated in the sauce. Cook for a further 5–7 minutes or until heated through and the sauce has thickened, stirring frequently. Season with salt and pepper to taste and sprinkle with the remaining mint and sliced scallions. Serve immediately.

Step *1*

Step *2*

Step *4*

Curried Roast Potatoes

This Indian-inspired dish would fit easily into any Western menu, or how about serving with a curry in place of the more traditional rice?

SERVES 4

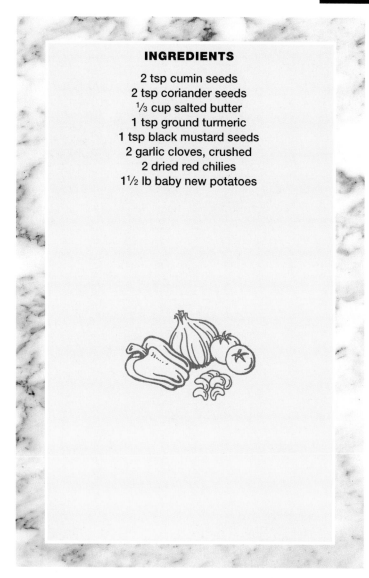

INGREDIENTS

2 tsp cumin seeds
2 tsp coriander seeds
⅓ cup salted butter
1 tsp ground turmeric
1 tsp black mustard seeds
2 garlic cloves, crushed
2 dried red chilies
1½ lb baby new potatoes

1 Grind the cumin and coriander seeds together with a pestle and mortar or spice grinder. Grinding them fresh like this captures all of the flavor before it has a chance to dry out.

2 Melt the butter gently in a roasting pan and add the turmeric, mustard seeds, garlic, chilies, and the ground cumin and coriander seeds. Stir well to combine evenly. Place in a preheated oven, 400°F, for 5 minutes.

3 Remove the pan from the oven – the spices should be very fragrant at this stage – and add the potatoes. Stir well so that the butter and spice mix coats the potatoes completely.

4 Put back in the preheated oven and bake for 20–25 minutes. Stir occasionally to ensure that the potatoes are coated evenly. Test the potatoes with a skewer – if they drop off the end of the skewer when lifted, they are done. Serve immediately.

Step *1*

Step *2*

Step *4*

Potato Fritters with Relish

These are incredibly simple to make and sure to be popular served as a tempting snack or as an accompaniment to almost any Indian main course dish.

MAKES 8

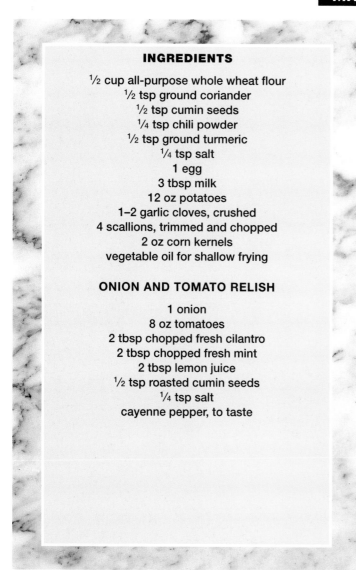

INGREDIENTS

½ cup all-purpose whole wheat flour
½ tsp ground coriander
½ tsp cumin seeds
¼ tsp chili powder
½ tsp ground turmeric
¼ tsp salt
1 egg
3 tbsp milk
12 oz potatoes
1–2 garlic cloves, crushed
4 scallions, trimmed and chopped
2 oz corn kernels
vegetable oil for shallow frying

ONION AND TOMATO RELISH

1 onion
8 oz tomatoes
2 tbsp chopped fresh cilantro
2 tbsp chopped fresh mint
2 tbsp lemon juice
½ tsp roasted cumin seeds
¼ tsp salt
cayenne pepper, to taste

1 First make the relish. Cut the onion and tomatoes into small dice and place in a bowl with the remaining ingredients. Mix well and leave to stand for at least 15 minutes before serving to allow the flavors to blend.

2 Place the flour in a bowl, stir in the spices and salt, and make a well in the center. Add the egg and milk and mix to form a fairly thick batter.

3 Coarsely grate the potatoes, place in a strainer, and rinse well under cold running water. Drain and squeeze dry, then stir into the batter with the garlic, scallions, and corn.

4 Heat about ¼ in. oil in a large skillet and add a few tablespoonfuls of the mixture at a time, flattening each one to form a thin cake. Fry gently for 2–3 minutes or until golden brown and cooked through, turning frequently.

5 Drain on paper towels and keep hot while frying the remaining mixture in the same way. Serve hot with onion and tomato relish.

Step *1*

Step *2*

Step *5*

Aloo Chat

Aloo Chat (chat means salad) is one of a variety of Indian foods served at any time of the day, to satisfy and stimulate the appetite.

SERVES 4

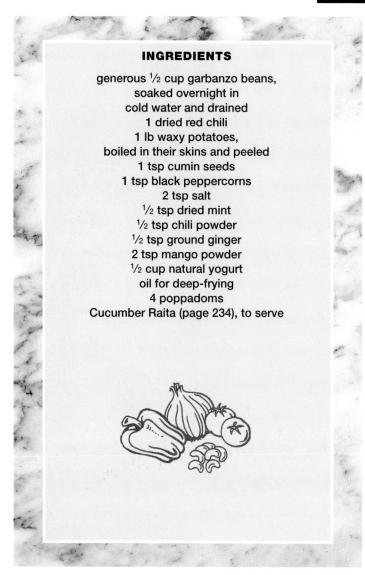

INGREDIENTS

generous ½ cup garbanzo beans,
soaked overnight in
cold water and drained
1 dried red chili
1 lb waxy potatoes,
boiled in their skins and peeled
1 tsp cumin seeds
1 tsp black peppercorns
2 tsp salt
½ tsp dried mint
½ tsp chili powder
½ tsp ground ginger
2 tsp mango powder
½ cup natural yogurt
oil for deep-frying
4 poppadoms
Cucumber Raita (page 234), to serve

1 Boil the garbanzo beans with the chili in plenty of water for about 1 hour until tender. Drain.

2 Cut the potatoes into 1 in. dice and mix with the garbanzo beans while they are still warm. Set aside.

3 Grind together the cumin, peppercorns, and salt in a spice grinder or with a pestle and mortar. Stir in the mint, chili powder, ginger, and mango powder.

4 Put a small dry saucepan or skillet over a low heat and add the spice mix. Stir until fragrant, then immediately remove from the heat.

5 Stir half of the spice mix into the garbanzo beans and potatoes, and stir the rest into the yogurt.

6 Cook the poppadoms according to the pack instructions. Drain on plenty of paper towels. Break into bite-size pieces and stir into the potatoes and garbanzo beans. Spoon over the spiced yogurt and serve with the cucumber raita.

Step *1*

Step *2*

Step *4*

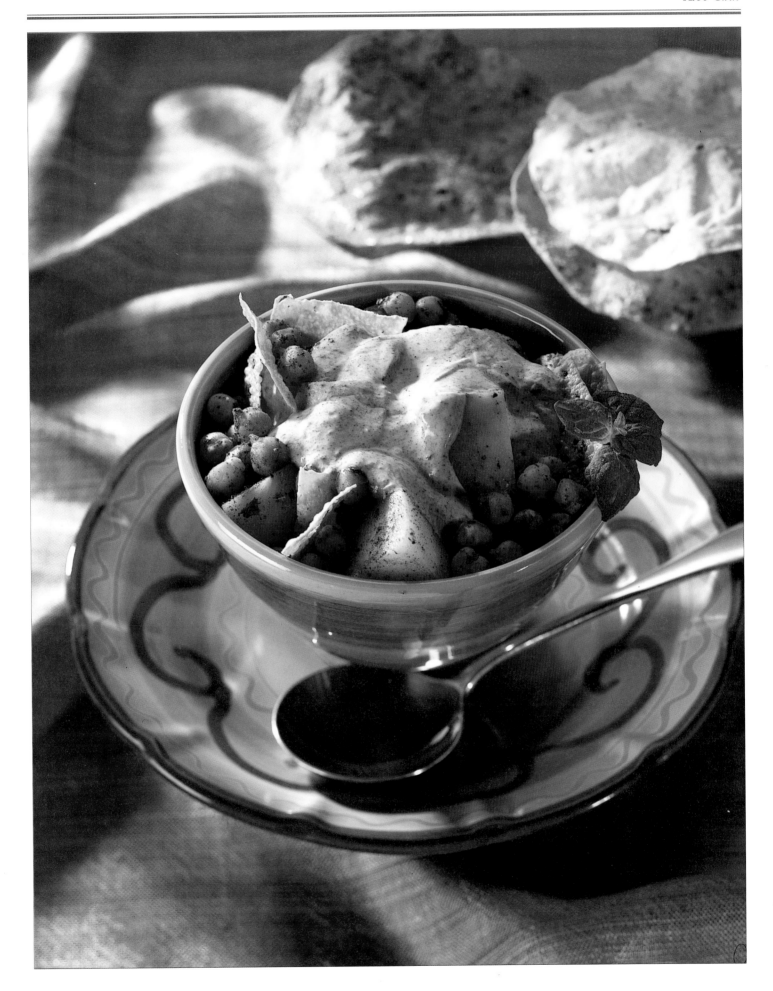

Muttar Paneer

Paneer is a delicious fresh, soft cheese frequently used in Indian cooking. It is easily made at home, but remember to make it the day before required.

SERVES 6

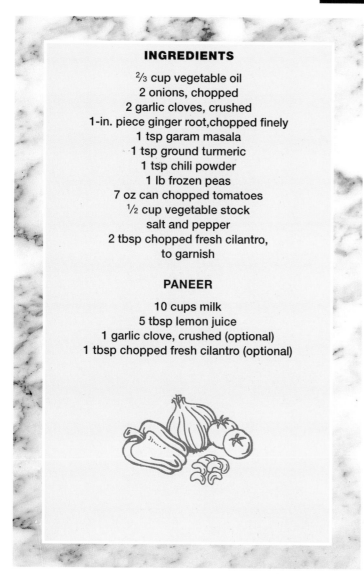

INGREDIENTS

⅔ cup vegetable oil
2 onions, chopped
2 garlic cloves, crushed
1-in. piece ginger root, chopped finely
1 tsp garam masala
1 tsp ground turmeric
1 tsp chili powder
1 lb frozen peas
7 oz can chopped tomatoes
½ cup vegetable stock
salt and pepper
2 tbsp chopped fresh cilantro,
to garnish

PANEER

10 cups milk
5 tbsp lemon juice
1 garlic clove, crushed (optional)
1 tbsp chopped fresh cilantro (optional)

1 To make the paneer, bring the milk to a rolling boil in a large saucepan. Remove from the heat and stir in the lemon juice. Return to the heat for about 1 minute until the curds and whey separate. Remove from the heat. Line a colander with double thickness of cheesecloth and pour the mixture through the cheesecloth, adding the garlic and cilantro, if using. Squeeze all the liquid from the curds and leave to drain.

2 Transfer to a dish, cover with a plate and weights, and leave overnight in the refrigerator.

3 Cut the pressed paneer into small cubes. Heat the oil in a large skillet, add the paneer cubes, and fry until golden on all sides. Remove from the skillet and drain on paper towels.

4 Pour off some of the oil, leaving about 4 tablespoons in the skillet. Add the onions, garlic, and ginger and fry gently for about 5 minutes, stirring frequently. Stir in the spices and fry gently for 2 minutes. Add the peas, tomatoes, and stock, and season with salt and pepper. Cover and simmer for 10 minutes, stirring occasionally, until the onion is tender.

5 Add the fried paneer cubes and cook for a further 5 minutes. Taste and adjust the seasoning, if necessary. Sprinkle with the cilantro and serve at once.

Step *1*

Step *4*

Step *5*

Palak Paneer

Paneer, curd cheese, features widely on Indian menus. It is combined with all sorts of ingredients, but most popularly with spinach and vegetables.

SERVES 4–6

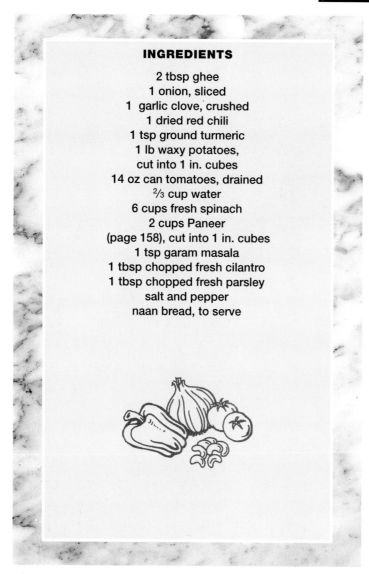

INGREDIENTS

2 tbsp ghee
1 onion, sliced
1 garlic clove, crushed
1 dried red chili
1 tsp ground turmeric
1 lb waxy potatoes,
cut into 1 in. cubes
14 oz can tomatoes, drained
²⁄₃ cup water
6 cups fresh spinach
2 cups Paneer
(page 158), cut into 1 in. cubes
1 tsp garam masala
1 tbsp chopped fresh cilantro
1 tbsp chopped fresh parsley
salt and pepper
naan bread, to serve

1 Heat the ghee in a saucepan, add the onion, and cook over a low heat for 10 minutes until very soft. Add the garlic and chili and cook for a further 5 minutes.

2 Add the turmeric, salt, potatoes, tomatoes, and water and bring to a boil.

3 Simmer for 10–15 minutes until the potatoes are cooked.

4 Stir in the spinach, cheese cubes, garam masala, cilantro, and parsley, and season to taste.

5 Simmer for a further 5 minutes and season well. Serve with naan bread.

Step *1*

Step *2*

Step *4*

RICE DISHES

Rice is a staple ingredient in India and has been used in cooking for thousands of years. It is the first food that a new Indian bride offers her husband; it is also the first food offered to a new-born baby.

Despite the mystique and ritual surrounding the cooking of rice, it is one of the most straightforward grains to prepare. A bowl of fluffy rice, delicately flavored with mild spices, is served at virtually every main meal in India, and acts as a filling base and a foil for the richer, spicier dishes.

The stunning mountain ranges that are the Himalayas provide the crystal-clear mineral water that is used to grow basmati rice. For basmati rice to be classified as such, it must be grown in the foothills of the Himalayas. However, it is such a desirable commodity in the world market that due to 'creative' sales techniques, more 'basmati' rice is sold each year than is harvested! Described as the 'prince of rice', basmati rice has a greater fragrance and a nuttier taste than ordinary long-grain rice, and it has a longer, more slender grain.

Aromatic Pilau

This rice dish forms the perfect accompaniment to most main courses. It can be prepared ahead of time and reheated in the microwave oven just before serving.

SERVES 4–5

INGREDIENTS

1¼ cups basmati rice
2 tbsp ghee or vegetable oil
1 onion, chopped
3 cardamom pods, crushed
3 black peppercorns
3 cloves
1 tsp cumin seeds
½ cinnamon stick or piece of cassia bark
½ tsp ground turmeric
2½ cups boiling water or stock
⅓ cup seedless raisins or golden raisins
2 oz frozen peas
¼ cup slivered almonds, toasted
crisp fried onion rings (optional), to garnish
salt and pepper

1 Place the rice in a strainer and wash well under cold running water until the water runs clear. Drain well.

2 Heat the oil in a large saucepan, add the onion and spices, and fry gently for 1 minute, stirring all the time. Stir in the rice and mix well until coated in the spiced oil, then add the boiling water or stock, and season with salt and pepper to taste.

3 Bring to a boil, stir well, then cover, reduce the heat, and cook gently for 15 minutes without uncovering. Add the raisins and peas, re-cover, and leave to stand for 15 minutes.

4 Uncover, fluff up with a fork, and stir the toasted slivered almonds into the mixture. Serve hot, garnished with crisp fried onion rings, if liked.

Step *2*

Step *3*

Step *4*

Spiced Basmati Pilau

Omit the broccoli and mushrooms from this recipe if you require only a simple spiced pilau. Remove the whole spices before serving.

SERVES 6

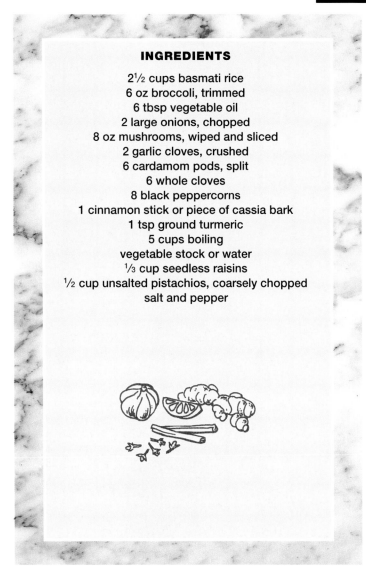

INGREDIENTS

2½ cups basmati rice
6 oz broccoli, trimmed
6 tbsp vegetable oil
2 large onions, chopped
8 oz mushrooms, wiped and sliced
2 garlic cloves, crushed
6 cardamom pods, split
6 whole cloves
8 black peppercorns
1 cinnamon stick or piece of cassia bark
1 tsp ground turmeric
5 cups boiling
vegetable stock or water
⅓ cup seedless raisins
½ cup unsalted pistachios, coarsely chopped
salt and pepper

1 Place the rice in a strainer and wash well under cold running water until the water runs clear. Drain. Trim off most of the broccoli stalk and cut into small flowerets, then quarter the stalk lengthwise, and cut diagonally into ½-in. pieces.

2 Heat the oil in a large saucepan, add the onions and broccoli stalks, and cook gently for 3 minutes, stirring frequently. Add the mushrooms, rice, garlic, and spices and cook gently for 1 minute, stirring frequently until the rice is coated in spiced oil.

3 Add the boiling stock and season with salt and pepper. Stir in the broccoli flowerets and bring the mixture back to a boil. Cover, reduce the heat, and cook gently for 15 minutes without uncovering.

4 Remove from the heat and leave to stand for 5 minutes without uncovering. Add the raisins and pistachios and gently fork through to fluff up the grains. Serve hot.

Step *1*

Step *3*

Step *4*

Shrimp Pilau

This is an Arabian-inspired creation, reminiscent of the spice trade of Sri Lanka. Serve it at family meals, sophisticated dinner parties, and buffets.

SERVES 4–6

INGREDIENTS

1-in. piece ginger root, chopped finely
4 garlic cloves, crushed
3 green chilies, deseeded and chopped
1 tsp cumin seeds
2 tsp coriander seeds
2 tbsp oil
2 shallots, chopped finely
generous 1 cup basmati rice
10 cloves
2-in. piece cinnamon stick
5 cardamom pods
1 bay leaf
½ cup coconut milk
1¾ cups fish stock
1 cup cooked, peeled shrimp
2 tbsp cashew nuts, chopped and toasted
2 tbsp chopped fresh cilantro
2 tbsp grated or shredded
coconut, toasted
lemon and tomato wedges, to garnish

1 Grind together the ginger, garlic, and green chilies in a coffee grinder or with a pestle and mortar.

2 Toast the cumin and coriander seeds and then grind them also.

3 Heat the oil in a wok or large skillet. Add the shallots and cook over a medium heat until soft, about 5 minutes. Add the garlic mixture and stir until fragrant, about 1 minute. Add the cumin and coriander. Add the rice and stir until translucent.

4 Put the cloves, cinnamon, cardamom, and bay leaf into a piece of cheesecloth. This is not essential but it makes them easier to remove at the end. Add the bag of spices to the pan.

5 Stir in the coconut milk and fish stock. Bring to a boil, stir once, and simmer for 15–18 minutes, or until all the liquid is absorbed.

6 Add the shrimp, cashew nuts, and cilantro. Cover with a close-fitting lid or a piece of foil, reduce the heat to the lowest setting, and leave undisturbed for 10 minutes.

7 Discard the cheesecloth bag of spices. Transfer the pilau to a serving dish and fork through lightly. Sprinkle over the toasted coconut and garnish with the lemon and tomato wedges.

Step *2*

Step *4*

Step *6*

Hyderabad Rice Pilau

This is a wonderfully colorful pilau, full of spice and flavor and aromatic ingredients, from exotic okra to saffron and hot cayenne.

SERVES 6

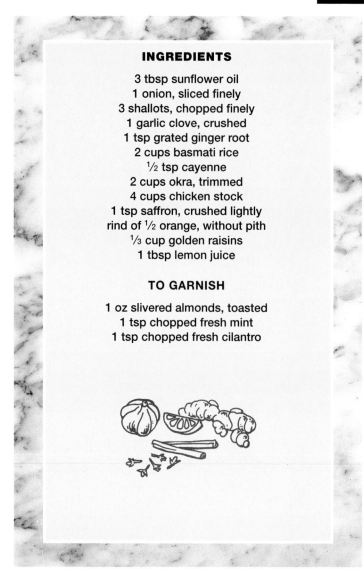

INGREDIENTS

3 tbsp sunflower oil
1 onion, sliced finely
3 shallots, chopped finely
1 garlic clove, crushed
1 tsp grated ginger root
2 cups basmati rice
½ tsp cayenne
2 cups okra, trimmed
4 cups chicken stock
1 tsp saffron, crushed lightly
rind of ½ orange, without pith
⅓ cup golden raisins
1 tbsp lemon juice

TO GARNISH

1 oz slivered almonds, toasted
1 tsp chopped fresh mint
1 tsp chopped fresh cilantro

1 Heat the oil in a wok or large skillet until quite hot. Fry the onions until golden brown, then remove, and drain on paper towels. Do not cook them all at once, as they won't be crisp.

2 Reduce the heat. Cook the shallots in the remaining oil until soft, about 5 minutes. Add the garlic and ginger, and stir. Stir in the rice, cayenne, and okra.

3 Pour in the chicken stock, and add the saffron and orange rind. Bring to a boil and simmer over a moderate heat for 15 minutes.

4 Add the golden raisins at the end of this time and stir in the lemon juice.

5 Remove the piece of orange rind if you prefer, then transfer to a serving dish, and garnish with the fried onion, toasted almonds, mint, and cilantro.

Step *1*

Step *3*

Step *4*

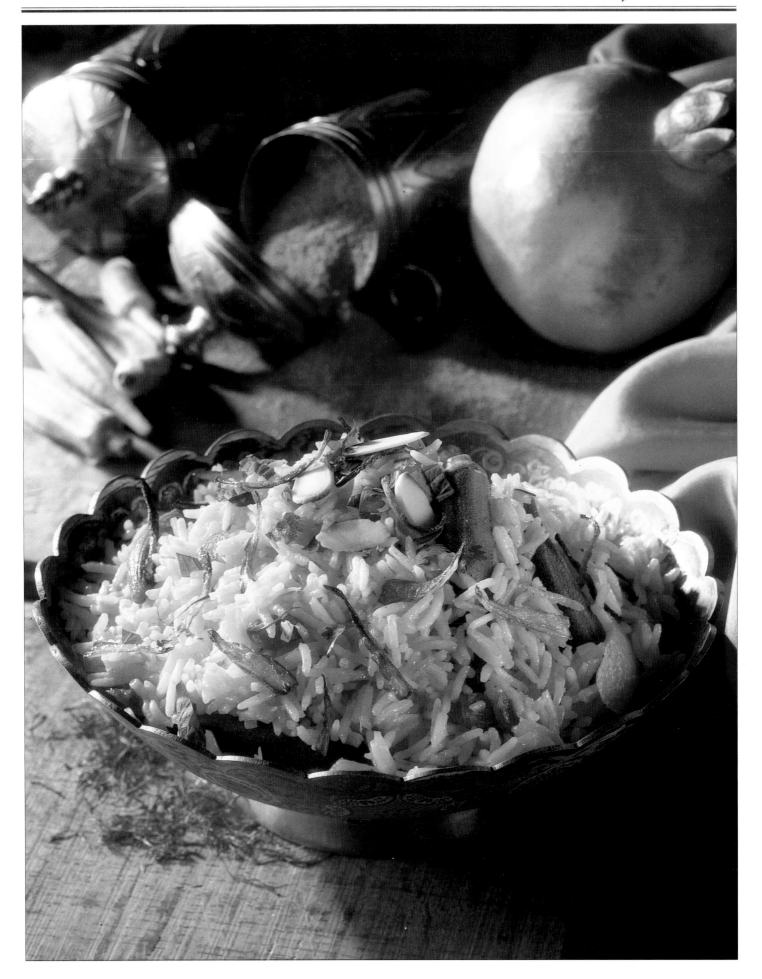

Aromatic Basmati Rice & Saffron Rice

For the best results when cooking basmati rice, rinse the raw rice under the tap and then soak in cold water for 30 minutes.

SERVES 4

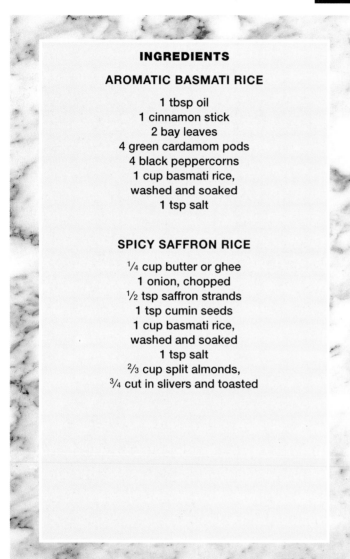

INGREDIENTS

AROMATIC BASMATI RICE

1 tbsp oil
1 cinnamon stick
2 bay leaves
4 green cardamom pods
4 black peppercorns
1 cup basmati rice,
washed and soaked
1 tsp salt

SPICY SAFFRON RICE

¼ cup butter or ghee
1 onion, chopped
½ tsp saffron strands
1 tsp cumin seeds
1 cup basmati rice,
washed and soaked
1 tsp salt
⅔ cup split almonds,
¾ cut in slivers and toasted

1 To make the aromatic rice, heat the oil in a heavy-based saucepan and fry the cinnamon, bay leaves, cardamom pods, and black peppercorns for 30 seconds.

2 Add the rice, salt, and enough water to cover the rice by 1 in. Cover with a tight-fitting lid, bring to a boil, and simmer for 20 minutes or until all the water has been absorbed and the rice is tender.

3 To make the saffron rice, heat the butter or ghee in a heavy-based saucepan, add the onion, and stir-fry. Add the saffron strands and cumin seeds and fry for 30 seconds.

4 Add the rice and fry for 2 minutes until it has absorbed the oil and the saffron color.

5 Add the salt and enough water to cover the rice by 1 in. Cover with a tight-fitting lid and simmer for 20 minutes until all the water has been absorbed and the rice is tender. Stir in the almonds.

Step *1*

Step *2*

Step *4*

Brown Rice with Fruit & Nuts

Here is a tasty and filling rice dish that is nice and spicy and includes fruits for a refreshing flavor and toasted nuts for an interesting crunchy texture.

SERVES 4–6

INGREDIENTS

4 tbsp vegetable ghee or oil
1 large onion, chopped
2 garlic cloves, crushed
1-in. piece ginger root,
chopped finely
1 tsp chili powder
1 tsp cumin seeds
1 tbsp mild or medium
curry powder or paste
1½ cups brown rice
3½ cups boiling
vegetable stock
14 oz can chopped tomatoes
6 oz no-need-to-soak dried apricots
or peaches, cut into slivers
1 red bell pepper, cored,
deseeded and diced
3 oz frozen peas
1–2 small, slightly green bananas
⅓–½ cup toasted mixed nuts
salt and pepper
sprigs of cilantro, to garnish

1 Heat the ghee or oil in a large saucepan, add the onion, and fry gently for 3 minutes. Stir in the garlic, ginger, spices, and rice. Cook gently for 2 minutes, stirring all the time until the rice is coated in the spiced oil.

2 Pour in the boiling stock. Add the tomatoes and season with salt and pepper to taste. Bring to a boil, then reduce the heat, cover, and simmer gently for 40 minutes or until the rice is almost cooked and most of the liquid is absorbed.

3 Add the apricots or peaches, red bell pepper, and peas. Cover and continue cooking for 10 minutes. Remove from the heat and allow to stand for 5 minutes without uncovering.

4 Peel and slice the bananas. Uncover the rice mixture and toss with a fork to mix. Add the toasted nuts and sliced banana and toss lightly. Transfer to a warm serving platter and garnish with sprigs of cilantro. Serve hot.

Step *1*

Step *3*

Step *4*

Shrimp Biryani

Like Lamb Biryani (page 180), this dish is usually served on special occasions because it needs close attention during cooking.

SERVES 6–8

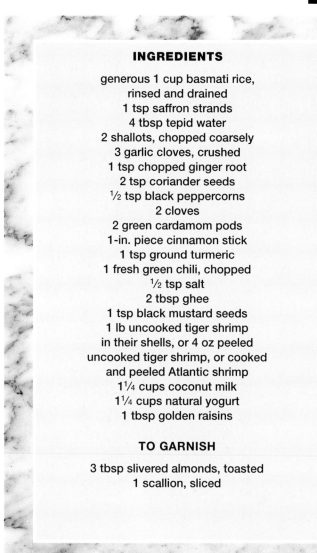

INGREDIENTS

generous 1 cup basmati rice,
rinsed and drained
1 tsp saffron strands
4 tbsp tepid water
2 shallots, chopped coarsely
3 garlic cloves, crushed
1 tsp chopped ginger root
2 tsp coriander seeds
½ tsp black peppercorns
2 cloves
2 green cardamom pods
1-in. piece cinnamon stick
1 tsp ground turmeric
1 fresh green chili, chopped
½ tsp salt
2 tbsp ghee
1 tsp black mustard seeds
1 lb uncooked tiger shrimp
in their shells, or 4 oz peeled
uncooked tiger shrimp, or cooked
and peeled Atlantic shrimp
1¼ cups coconut milk
1¼ cups natural yogurt
1 tbsp golden raisins

TO GARNISH

3 tbsp slivered almonds, toasted
1 scallion, sliced

1 Soak the rice in cold water for 30 minutes. Combine the saffron with the water and soak for 10 minutes.

2 Put the shallots, garlic, ginger, coriander, peppercorns, cloves, cardamom, cinnamon, turmeric, chili, and salt in a spice grinder and grind to a paste or use a pestle and mortar.

3 Heat the ghee in a large saucepan and add the mustard seeds. When they start to pop, add the shrimp and stir over a high heat for 1 minute. Stir in the spice mix.

4 Add the coconut milk and yogurt, and simmer for 20 minutes.

5 Meanwhile, bring a large saucepan of salted water to a boil. Drain the rice and slowly add to the pan. Boil for 12 minutes. Drain. Carefully pile the rice on the shrimp. Spoon over the golden raisins and trickle the saffron infusion in lines over the rice.

6 Cover the pan with a clean dishcloth and put the lid on tightly. Remove the pan from heat and leave to stand for 5 minutes to infuse. Serve, garnished with the toasted almonds and scallion.

Step *3*

Step *4*

Step *6*

Lentil & Vegetable Biryani

*A delicious mix of vegetables, basmati rice, and lentils produces a
wholesome and nutritious dish.*

SERVES 6

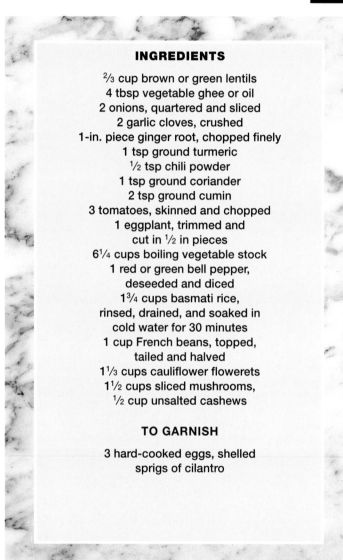

INGREDIENTS

⅔ cup brown or green lentils
4 tbsp vegetable ghee or oil
2 onions, quartered and sliced
2 garlic cloves, crushed
1-in. piece ginger root, chopped finely
1 tsp ground turmeric
½ tsp chili powder
1 tsp ground coriander
2 tsp ground cumin
3 tomatoes, skinned and chopped
1 eggplant, trimmed and
cut in ½ in pieces
6¼ cups boiling vegetable stock
1 red or green bell pepper,
deseeded and diced
1¾ cups basmati rice,
rinsed, drained, and soaked in
cold water for 30 minutes
1 cup French beans, topped,
tailed and halved
1⅓ cups cauliflower flowerets
1½ cups sliced mushrooms,
½ cup unsalted cashews

TO GARNISH

3 hard-cooked eggs, shelled
sprigs of cilantro

1 Rinse the lentils under cold running water and drain. Heat the ghee or oil in a saucepan, add the onions, and fry gently for 2 minutes. Stir in the garlic, ginger, and spices and fry gently for 1 minute, stirring frequently.

2 Stir in the lentils, tomatoes, eggplant, and 2½ cups of the stock. Cover and simmer gently for 20 minutes. Add the red or green bell pepper and cook for a further 10 minutes or until the lentils are tender and all the liquid has been absorbed.

3 Drain the rice and put in another pan with the remaining stock. Bring to a boil, add the French beans, cauliflower, and mushrooms, then cover, and cook gently for 15 minutes or until the rice and vegetables are tender. Remove from the heat and leave to stand for 10 minutes, covered.

4 Add the lentil mixture and the cashews to the cooked rice and mix lightly. Pile onto a warm serving platter and garnish with wedges of hard-cooked egg and sprigs of cilantro. Serve hot.

Step *2*

Step *3*

Step *4*

Lamb Biryani

In India this elaborate, beautifully colored dish is usually served at parties and on festive occasions. This version can be made on any day, festive or not.

SERVES 4

INGREDIENTS

generous 1 cup basmati rice,
rinsed and soaked in cold
water for 30 minutes
½ tsp salt
2 garlic cloves, peeled and left whole
1-in. piece ginger root, grated
4 cloves
½ tsp black peppercorns
2 green cardamom pods
1 tsp cumin seeds
1 tsp coriander seeds
1-in. piece cinnamon stick
1 tsp saffron strands
4 tbsp tepid water
2 tbsp ghee
2 shallots, sliced
¼ tsp grated nutmeg
¼ tsp chili powder
1 lb boneless lamb, cut into
1 in. cubes
¾ cup natural yogurt
2 tbsp golden raisins
¼ cup slivered almonds, toasted

1 Bring a large saucepan of salted water to a boil. Add the rice and boil for 6 minutes. Drain and set aside.

2 Grind together the garlic, ginger, cloves, peppercorns, cardamom pods, cumin, coriander, and cinnamon.

3 Combine the saffron and water and set aside. Heat the ghee in a large saucepan and add the shallots. Fry until golden brown, then add the ground spice mix, nutmeg, and chili powder. Stir for 1 minute and add the lamb. Cook until evenly browned.

4 Add the yogurt, stirring constantly, then the golden raisins, and bring to a simmer. Cook for 40 minutes, stirring occasionally.

5 Carefully pile the rice on the sauce, in a pyramid shape. Trickle the saffron infusion over the rice in lines. Cover the pan with a clean dishcloth and put on the lid. Reduce the heat to low and cook for 10 minutes. Remove the lid and dishcloth, and quickly make 3 holes in the rice with a wooden spoon handle, to the level of the sauce, but not touching it. Replace the dishcloth and the lid and leave to stand for 5 minutes.

6 Remove the lid and dishcloth, lightly fork the rice, and serve, sprinkled with the toasted almonds.

Step *1*

Step *3*

Step *5*

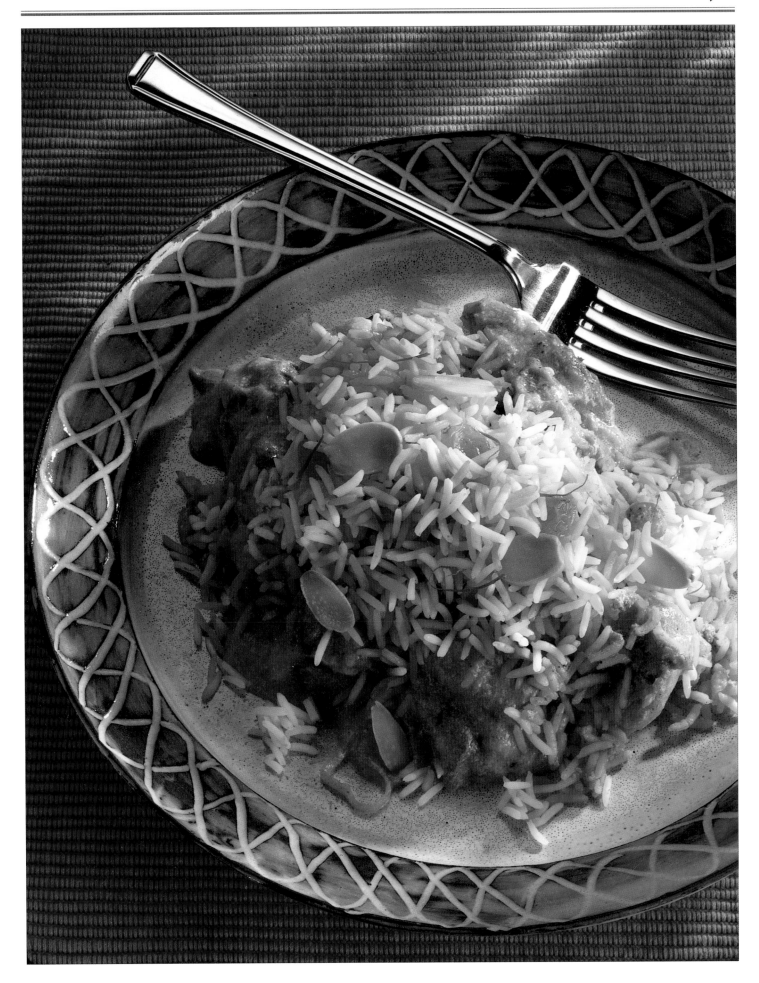

Kitchouri

This is the dish from which kedgeree evolved. The British colonists adopted it, adding preserved fish, to make the version we know today.

SERVES 4

INGREDIENTS

2 tbsp ghee or butter
1 red onion, chopped finely
1 garlic clove, crushed
½ celery stalk, chopped finely
1 tsp turmeric
½ tsp garam masala
1 green chili, deseeded and chopped finely
½ tsp cumin seeds
1 tbsp chopped fresh cilantro
generous ½ cup basmati rice, rinsed and soaked in cold water for 30 minutes
½ cup green lentils
1¼ cups vegetable juice
2½ cups vegetable stock

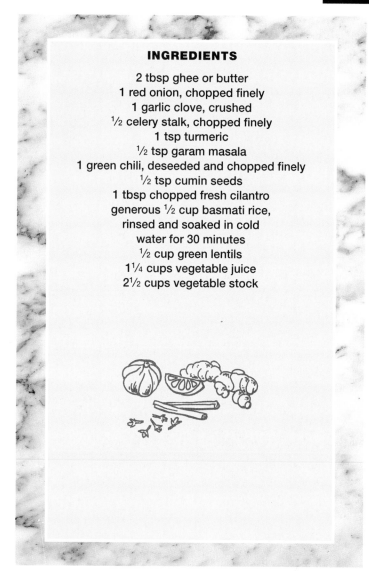

1 Melt the ghee in a large saucepan. Add the onion, garlic, and celery, and cook until soft, about 5 minutes.

2 Add the turmeric, garam masala, chili, cumin seeds, and cilantro. Stir until fragrant over a moderate heat, about 1 minute.

3 Add the rice and lentils. Stir until the rice is translucent, about 1 minute.

4 Pour the vegetable juice and vegetable stock into the saucepan, and bring to a boil. Cover and simmer over a low heat for about 20 minutes, stirring occasionally, or until the lentils are tender.

5 Transfer to a warm serving dish and serve hot.

Step *1*

Step *2*

Step *4*

Coconut Rice

A delicious rice dish flavored with coconut and lemon. For a luxurious touch you can fork in a few shelled, chopped pistachios at the final stage.

SERVES 4–5

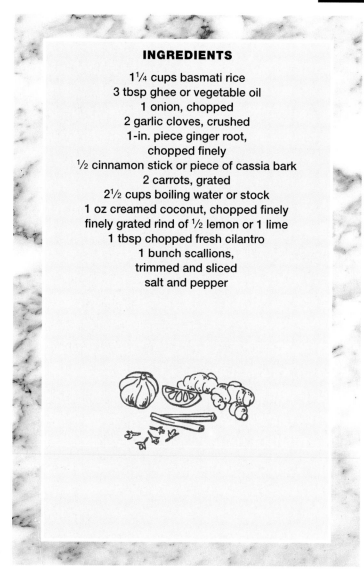

INGREDIENTS

1¼ cups basmati rice
3 tbsp ghee or vegetable oil
1 onion, chopped
2 garlic cloves, crushed
1-in. piece ginger root,
chopped finely
½ cinnamon stick or piece of cassia bark
2 carrots, grated
2½ cups boiling water or stock
1 oz creamed coconut, chopped finely
finely grated rind of ½ lemon or 1 lime
1 tbsp chopped fresh cilantro
1 bunch scallions,
trimmed and sliced
salt and pepper

1 Place the rice in a strainer and wash well under cold running water until the water runs clear. Drain well, then soak in cold water for 30 minutes, and drain again.

2 Heat the ghee or oil in a large saucepan, add the onion, garlic, ginger, and cinnamon, and fry gently for 1 minute. Stir in the rice and grated carrots and mix until well coated with the oil.

3 Stir in the water or stock and season with salt and pepper. Bring to a boil, cover, reduce the heat, and simmer gently for 15 minutes without taking off the lid.

4 Add the creamed coconut, lemon rind, chopped cilantro, and scallions, fork through, and serve immediately.

Step *2*

Step *3*

Step *4*

Saffron Rice

This is the classic way to serve rice, paired with saffron, so that each brings out the best in the other.

SERVES 8

INGREDIENTS

12 saffron threads, crushed lightly
2 tbsp warm water
1¾ cups water
1¼ cups basmati rice,
rinsed and soaked in cold
water for 30 minutes
1 tbsp slivered almonds, toasted

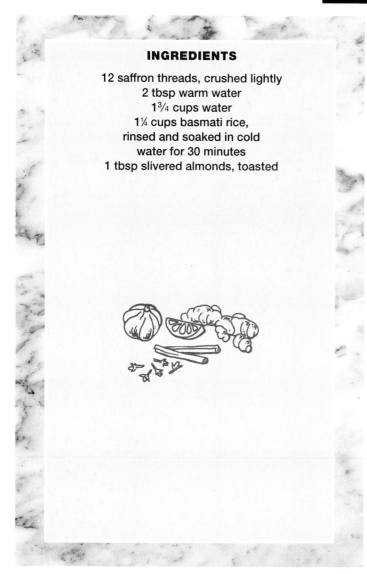

1 Put the saffron threads into a bowl with the warm water and leave for 10 minutes. They need to be crushed before soaking to ensure that the maximum flavor and color is extracted at this stage.

2 Put the water and rice into a medium saucepan and set it over the heat to boil. Stir in the saffron infusion.

3 Bring back to a gentle boil, stir again, and let the rice simmer, uncovered, for about 10 minutes, until all the water has been absorbed.

4 Cover tightly, reduce the heat to a very low heat, and leave for 10 minutes. Do not remove the lid. This method ensures that the grains separate and that the rice is not soggy.

5 Remove from the heat and transfer to a serving dish. Fork through the rice gently and sprinkle on the toasted almonds before serving.

Step *1*

Step *2*

Step *5*

PULSE DISHES

It is true, in the south of India at least, that Hindus are predominately vegetarian. In the north they are influenced by their Muslim and Persian neighbors, and more of the northern Hindus eat meat. But wherever you are in India, the meat is not always the tender, succulent product that we have come to expect in the West. This protein source often has to be supplemented, and there is a huge range and variety of pulses – dals – available.

Many Indians – and for that matter visitors to India – do survive on rice and dal or some sort of lentil stew for days or even weeks. Although it seems an unvaried diet, it is nourishing and quite satisfying.

Thali is one of the ways in which rice and dal are eaten; it takes its name from the tray on which the dish is served – a round metal tray holding six or seven small metal dishes (katoris) around the edge, leaving room for a large pile of rice in the middle. This southern Indian dish will usually have two or three dals, a curried vegetable, relishes, chutney, and a few poppadoms, and they are especially tasty. A thali is standard Indian railroad fare, appearing magically fresh and hot as it is served to hundreds of passengers en route.

Yellow Split Pea Casserole

*If ever there was a winter warmer, this is it – an intensely satisfying dish,
ideal for serving with a lightweight main dish, such as pilau or biryani.*

SERVES 6

INGREDIENTS

2 tbsp ghee
1 tsp black mustard seeds
1 onion, chopped finely
2 garlic cloves, crushed
1 carrot, grated
1-in. piece ginger root, grated
1 green chili, deseeded and chopped finely
1 tbsp tomato paste
1 cup yellow split peas,
soaked in water for 2 hours and drained
14 oz can chopped tomatoes
2 cups vegetable stock
1½ cups cubed pumpkin
8 oz cauliflower, cut into flowerets
2 tbsp oil
1 large eggplant, cubed
1 tbsp chopped fresh cilantro
1 tsp garam masala
salt and pepper

1 Melt the ghee over a medium heat in a large pan. Add the mustard seeds, and when they start to splutter, add the onion, garlic, carrot, and ginger. Cook until soft, about 5 minutes. Add the chili and stir in the tomato paste. Stir in the split peas.

2 Add the tomatoes and stock, and bring to a boil. Season well.

3 Simmer for 40 minutes, stirring occasionally. Add the pumpkin and cauliflower, and simmer for a further 30 minutes, covered, until the split peas are soft.

4 Meanwhile, heat the oil in a skillet over a high heat. Add the eggplant and stir until sealed on all sides. Remove and drain on paper towels.

5 Stir the eggplant into the split pea mixture with the cilantro and garam masala. Check for seasoning.

6 Transfer to a serving dish and serve immediately.

Step *1*

Step *3*

Step *4*

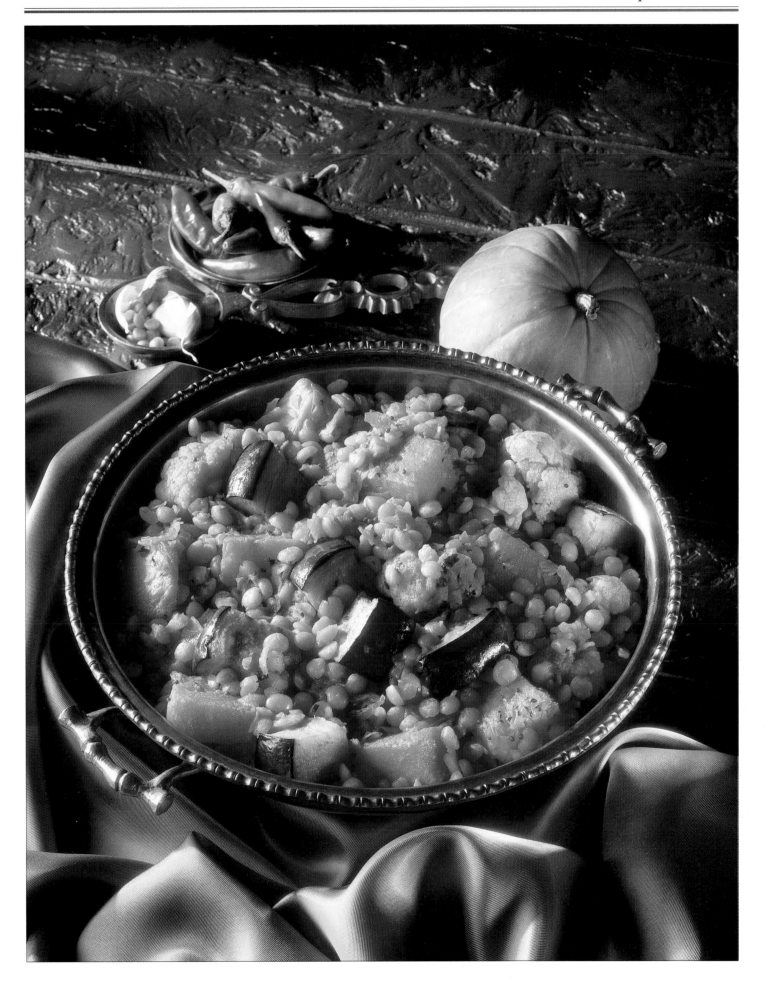

Split Peas with Vegetables

Here is a simple, yet nourishing and flavorful way of cooking yellow split peas. Vary the selection of vegetables and spices according to personal preferences.

SERVES 4–5

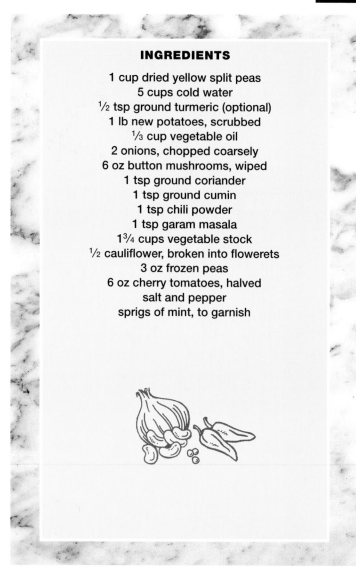

INGREDIENTS

1 cup dried yellow split peas
5 cups cold water
½ tsp ground turmeric (optional)
1 lb new potatoes, scrubbed
⅓ cup vegetable oil
2 onions, chopped coarsely
6 oz button mushrooms, wiped
1 tsp ground coriander
1 tsp ground cumin
1 tsp chili powder
1 tsp garam masala
1¾ cups vegetable stock
½ cauliflower, broken into flowerets
3 oz frozen peas
6 oz cherry tomatoes, halved
salt and pepper
sprigs of mint, to garnish

1 Place the split peas in a bowl, add the cold water, and leave to soak for at least 4 hours or overnight.

2 Place the peas and the soaking liquid in a fairly large saucepan, stir in the turmeric, if using, and bring to a boil. Skim off any surface scum, half-cover the pan with a lid, and simmer gently for 20 minutes or until the peas are tender and almost dry. Remove from the heat and reserve.

3 Meanwhile, cut the potatoes into ¼ in. thick slices. Heat the oil in a flameproof casserole, add the onions, potatoes, and mushrooms, and cook gently for 5 minutes, stirring frequently. Stir in the spices and fry gently for 1 minute, then add salt and pepper to taste, the stock, and the cauliflower flowerets.

4 Cover and simmer gently for 25 minutes or until the potato is tender, stirring occasionally. Add the split peas (and any of the cooking liquid) and the frozen peas. Bring to a boil, cover, and cook for 5 minutes.

5 Stir in the cherry tomatoes and cook for 2 minutes. Taste and adjust the seasoning, if necessary. Serve hot, garnished with sprigs of mint.

Step *2*

Step *3*

Step *5*

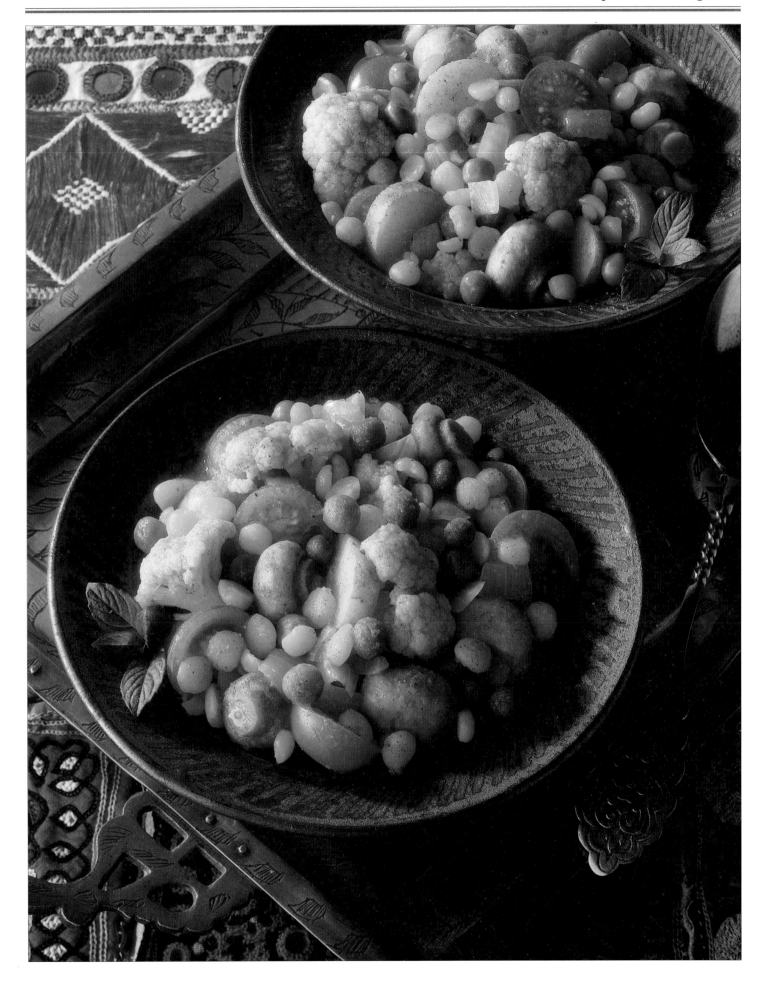

Channa Dal

This is a dish to consider next time you prepare a dal. Many types of dal (dried pulses and lentils) are used in India – yellow split peas are just one.

SERVES 4–6

INGREDIENTS

2 tbsp ghee
1 large onion, chopped finely
1 garlic clove, crushed
1 tbsp grated ginger root
1 tbsp cumin seeds, ground
2 tsp coriander seeds, ground
1 dried red chili
1-in. piece cinnamon stick
1 tsp salt
½ tsp ground turmeric
1 cup yellow split peas,
soaked in cold water for 1 hour and drained
14 oz can tomatoes
1¼ cups water
2 tsp garam masala

1 Heat the ghee in a large saucepan, add the onion, garlic, and ginger, and fry for 3–4 minutes until the onion has softened slightly.

2 Add the cumin, coriander, chili, cinnamon, salt, and turmeric, then stir in the split peas, and mix well.

3 Add the tomatoes, breaking them up slightly with the back of the spoon.

4 Add the water and bring to a boil. Reduce the heat to very low and simmer, uncovered, for about 40 minutes, stirring occasionally, until most of the liquid has been absorbed and the split peas are tender. Skim the surface occasionally with a perforated spoon to remove any scum.

5 Gradually stir in the garam masala, tasting after each addition, until it is of the required flavor.

Step *2*

Step *3*

Step *4*

Garbanzo Beans & Eggplant in Tomato Cream

Canned garbanzo beans are used in this dish, but you could use black-eye beans or red kidney beans instead.

SERVES 4

INGREDIENTS

1 large eggplant
2 zucchini
6 tbsp vegetable ghee or oil
1 large onion, quartered and sliced
2 garlic cloves, crushed
1–2 fresh green chilies,
deseeded and chopped,
or use 1–2 tsp ground chili (from a jar)
2 tsp ground coriander
2 tsp cumin seeds
1 tsp ground turmeric
1 tsp garam masala
14 oz can chopped tomatoes
1¼ cups vegetable stock or water
salt and pepper
15 oz can garbanzo beans,
drained and rinsed
2 tbsp chopped fresh mint
1⅔ cup heavy cream

1 Trim the leaf end off the eggplant and cut into cubes. Trim and slice the zucchini. Heat the ghee or oil in a saucepan and slowly fry the eggplant, zucchini, onion, garlic, and chilies for about 5 minutes, stirring frequently and adding a little more oil to the pan, if necessary.

2 Stir in the spices and cook for 30 seconds. Add the tomatoes, stock, and salt and pepper to taste. Cook for 10 minutes.

3 Add the garbanzo beans to the pan and continue cooking for a further 5 minutes.

4 Stir in the mint and cream and reheat gently. Taste and adjust the seasoning, if necessary. Serve hot with plain or pilau rice, or with parathas, if preferred.

Step *1*

Step *2*

Step *4*

Kabli Channa Sag

*Pulses such as garbanzo beans are widely used in India, and this satisfying,
earthy dish is characteristically easy to make and quite delicious.*

SERVES 6

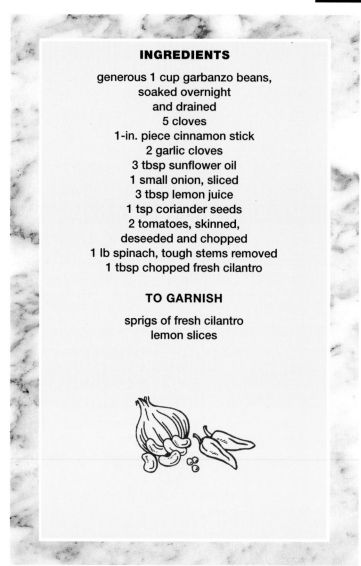

INGREDIENTS

generous 1 cup garbanzo beans,
soaked overnight
and drained
5 cloves
1-in. piece cinnamon stick
2 garlic cloves
3 tbsp sunflower oil
1 small onion, sliced
3 tbsp lemon juice
1 tsp coriander seeds
2 tomatoes, skinned,
deseeded and chopped
1 lb spinach, tough stems removed
1 tbsp chopped fresh cilantro

TO GARNISH

sprigs of fresh cilantro
lemon slices

1 Put the garbanzo beans into a saucepan with enough water to cover. Add the cloves, cinnamon, and 1 garlic clove that has been lightly crushed with the back of a knife to release the juices. Bring to a boil, reduce the heat, and simmer for 40–50 minutes, or until the garbanzo beans are tender. Skim off any foam that comes to the surface.

2 Meanwhile, heat 1 tablespoon of the oil in a saucepan. Crush the remaining garlic clove. Put this into the pan with the oil and the onion, and cook over a moderate heat until soft, about 5 minutes.

3 Remove the cloves, cinnamon, and garlic from the pan of garbanzo beans. Drain the garbanzo beans. Using a food processor or a fork, blend ½ cup of the garbanzo beans with the onion and garlic, the lemon juice, and 1 tablespoon of the oil until smooth. Stir this purée into the remaining garbanzo beans.

4 Heat the remaining oil in a large skillet, add the coriander seeds, and stir for 1 minute. Stir in the tomatoes, then add the spinach. Cover and cook for 1 minute over a moderate heat. The spinach should be wilted, but not soggy. Stir in the chopped cilantro and remove from the heat.

5 Transfer the garbanzo beans to a serving dish, and spoon over the spinach. Garnish with the cilantro and lemon.

Step *1*

Step *3*

Step *4*

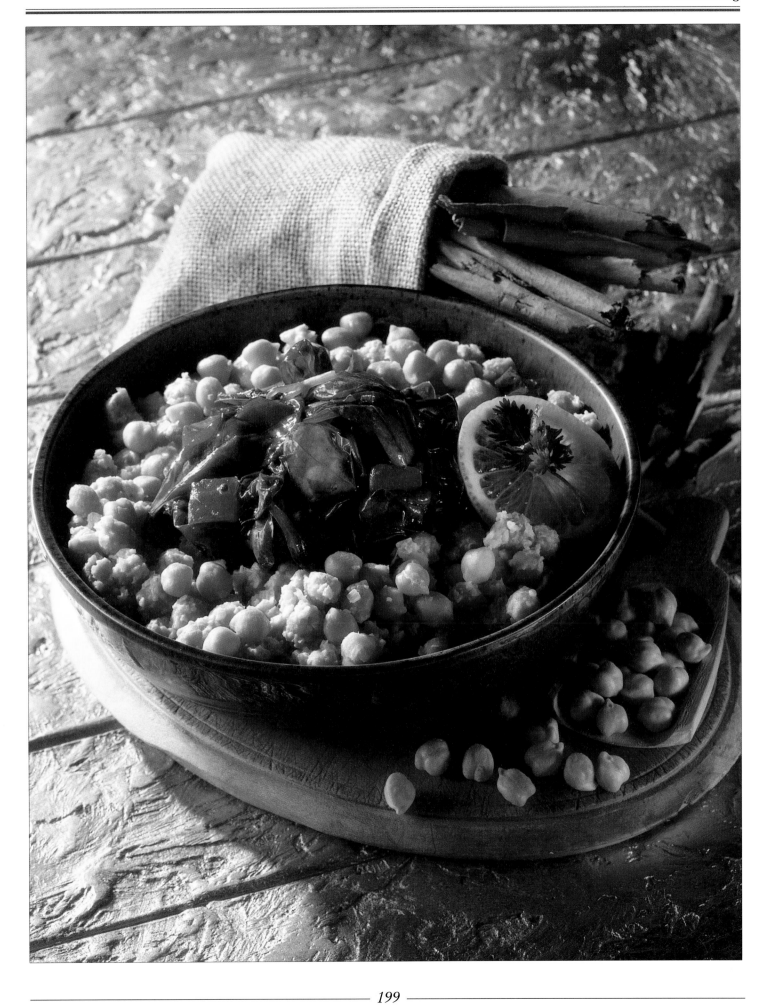

Egg & Lentil Curry

A nutritious meal that is easy and relatively quick to make. The curried lentil sauce would also be delicious served with cooked vegetables.

SERVES 4

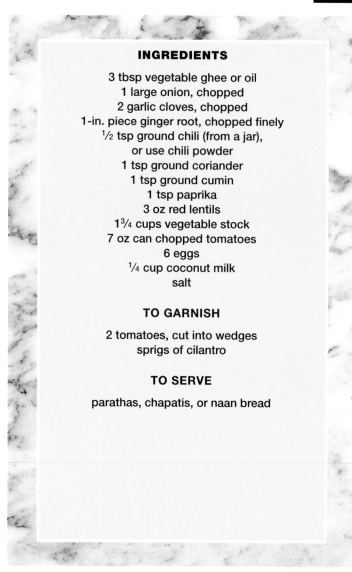

INGREDIENTS

3 tbsp vegetable ghee or oil
1 large onion, chopped
2 garlic cloves, chopped
1-in. piece ginger root, chopped finely
½ tsp ground chili (from a jar),
or use chili powder
1 tsp ground coriander
1 tsp ground cumin
1 tsp paprika
3 oz red lentils
1¾ cups vegetable stock
7 oz can chopped tomatoes
6 eggs
¼ cup coconut milk
salt

TO GARNISH

2 tomatoes, cut into wedges
sprigs of cilantro

TO SERVE

parathas, chapatis, or naan bread

1 Heat the ghee or oil in a saucepan, add the onion, and fry gently for 3 minutes. Stir in the garlic, ginger, chili, and spices and cook gently for 1 minute, stirring frequently. Stir in the lentils, stock, and chopped tomatoes and bring to a boil. Reduce the heat, cover, and simmer gently for 30 minutes, stirring occasionally until the lentils and onion are tender.

2 Meanwhile, put the eggs in a saucepan of cold water and bring to a boil. Reduce the heat and simmer for 10 minutes. Drain and cover immediately with cold water.

3 Stir the coconut milk into the lentil mixture and season well with salt to taste. Purée the mixture in a blender or food processor until smooth or push through a coarse strainer. Return to the pan and heat through.

4 Shell and cut the hard-cooked eggs in half lengthwise. Arrange 3 halves, in a petal design, on each serving plate. Spoon the hot lentil sauce over the eggs, adding enough to flood the serving plate. Arrange a tomato wedge and a sprig of cilantro between each halved egg. Serve hot with parathas, chapatis, or naan bread to mop up the sauce.

Step *1*

Step *3*

Step *4*

Tarka Dal

This is just one version of many dals that are served throughout India;
in the absence of regular supplies of meat, they form a staple part of the diet.

SERVES 4

INGREDIENTS

2 tbsp ghee
2 shallots, sliced
1 tsp yellow mustard seeds
2 garlic cloves, crushed
8 fenugreek seeds
½-in. piece ginger root, grated
½ tsp salt
½ cup red lentils
1 tbsp tomato paste
2½ cups water
2 tomatoes, skinned and chopped
1 tbsp lemon juice
4 tbsp chopped fresh cilantro
½ tsp chili powder
½ tsp garam masala
naan bread, to serve

1 Heat half the ghee in a large saucepan, and add the shallots. Cook for 2–3 minutes over a high heat, then add the mustard seeds. Cover the pan until the seeds begin to pop.

2 Immediately remove the lid from the pan and add the garlic, fenugreek, ginger, and salt.

3 Stir once and add the lentils, tomato paste, and water and simmer gently for 10 minutes.

4 Stir in the tomatoes, lemon juice, and cilantro and simmer for a further 4–5 minutes until the lentils are tender.

5 Transfer to a serving dish. Heat the remaining ghee in a small saucepan until it starts to bubble. Remove from the heat and stir in the garam masala and chili powder. Immediately pour over the tarka dal and serve.

Step *1*

Step *2*

Step *3*

Dal with Spinach

Green lentils are cooked in a delicious blend of spinach, onion, garlic, and spices. Okra is known as bhindi, ladies' fingers and gumbo.

SERVES 4

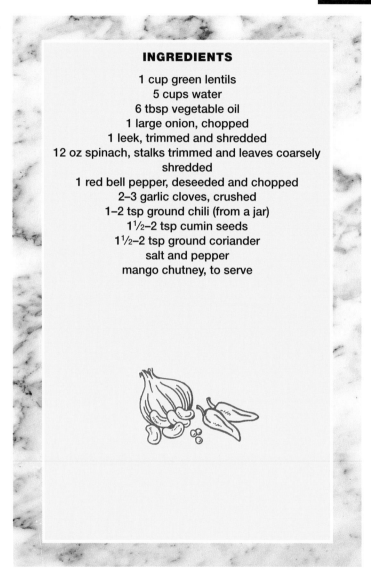

INGREDIENTS

1 cup green lentils
5 cups water
6 tbsp vegetable oil
1 large onion, chopped
1 leek, trimmed and shredded
12 oz spinach, stalks trimmed and leaves coarsely shredded
1 red bell pepper, deseeded and chopped
2–3 garlic cloves, crushed
1–2 tsp ground chili (from a jar)
1½–2 tsp cumin seeds
1½–2 tsp ground coriander
salt and pepper
mango chutney, to serve

1 Place the lentils in a strainer and rinse well under cold running water. Drain, then place in a saucepan with the water. Cover and cook for 30 minutes until the lentils are tender and the liquid has been absorbed.

2 Meanwhile, heat the oil in a large saucepan and add the onion, leek, spinach, and red bell pepper. Fry gently for 8 minutes, stirring and turning frequently until the spinach has wilted.

3 Stir in the garlic, chili, and spices and fry gently for a further 2 minutes.

4 When the lentils are cooked, uncover and shake the pan over a moderate heat for a few moments to dry off. Add the lentils to the spinach and onion mixture and toss together. Season with salt and pepper to taste and serve hot, with mango chutney.

Step *2*

Step *3*

Step *4*

Murkha Dal

With this dal recipe, the garlic is intended to burn in the bottom of the pan, so that the flavor permeates the dish.

SERVES 4

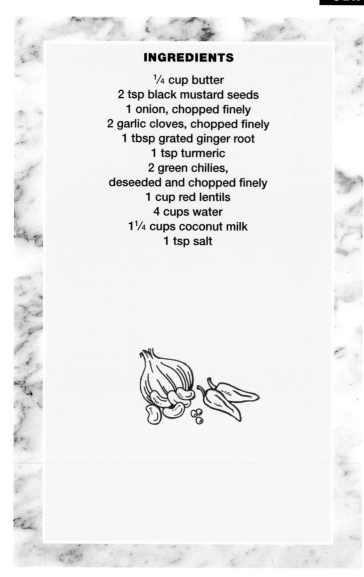

INGREDIENTS

¼ cup butter
2 tsp black mustard seeds
1 onion, chopped finely
2 garlic cloves, chopped finely
1 tbsp grated ginger root
1 tsp turmeric
2 green chilies,
deseeded and chopped finely
1 cup red lentils
4 cups water
1¼ cups coconut milk
1 tsp salt

1 Melt the butter in a large saucepan over a moderate heat. Add the mustard seeds and cover the pan. When you can hear the seeds popping, add the onion, garlic, and ginger. Cook, uncovered, until they are soft and the garlic is brown, about 7–8 minutes.

2 Stir in the turmeric and chilies and cook for 1–2 minutes until the chilies soften a little.

3 Add the lentils and cook for 2 minutes, stirring frequently, until the lentils begin to turn translucent.

4 Add the water, coconut milk, and salt. Stir well. Bring to a boil, then reduce the heat, and simmer for 40 minutes or until the desired consistency is reached. Cook the dal for longer if you prefer a thicker consistency. However, if you intend to reheat it later rather than eat it straightway, cook for only 30 minutes to allow for reheating time.

5 Serve immediately, while piping hot.

Step *1*

Step *3*

Step *4*

BREADS

Bread is another staple ingredient in India, used to mop up sauces and stews, and to make meals easier to eat with the hands. It is usually eaten hot, or within a few minutes of cooking.

With one or two exceptions, Indian breads are unleavened, that is they do not contain any rising agent. The flours are usually unrefined and often milled from grains other than wheat, including millet, barley, and white maize. Many people grind their flours at home simply by hand.

Since it is unleavened, Indian bread is very easy to make as it needs very little kneading and rising. Most breads are flat, usually circular in shape, often resembling griddle scones or pancakes. Some are dry-fried or fried with a little oil, others are deep-fried into wonderfully puffy hollow shells.

Breads appear in many forms – pooris, poppadoms, oven-baked naan, pan-fried chapatis, and parathas – all equally delicious.

Peshwari Naan

*A tandoor oven throws out a ferocious heat; for an authentic effect, leave
your broiler on for a long time before the first dough goes on.*

SERVES 4–6

INGREDIENTS

½ cup warm water
pinch of sugar
½ tsp active dried yeast
4 cups strong white flour
½ tsp salt
¼ cup natural yogurt
2 crisp, green apples, peeled, cooked, and puréed
⅓ cup golden raisins
½ cup slivered almonds
1 tbsp cilantro leaves
2 tbsp grated coconut

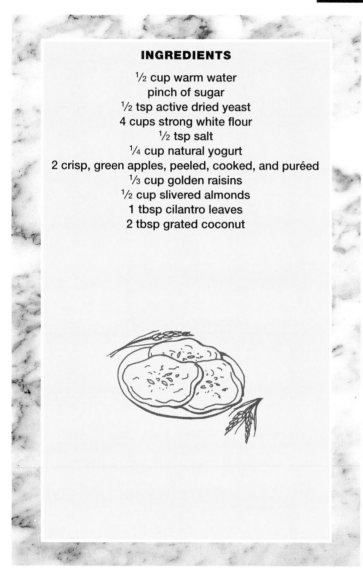

1 Combine the water and sugar in a bowl and sprinkle over the yeast. Leave for 5–10 minutes, until the yeast has dissolved and the mixture is foamy.

2 Put the flour and salt into a large bowl and make a well in the center. Add the yeast mixture and yogurt to the bowl. Draw the flour into the liquid, until all the flour is absorbed. Mix together, adding enough tepid water to form a soft dough, about ⅔ cup.

3 Turn out onto a floured board and knead for 10 minutes until smooth and elastic. Put into an oiled bowl, cover with a cloth, and leave for 3 hours in a warm place, or in the refrigerator overnight. Line the broiler pan with foil, shiny side up.

4 Divide the dough into 4 pieces and roll each piece out to an 8 in. oval.

5 Pull one end out into a teardrop shape, about ¼ in. thick. Lay on a floured surface and prick all over with a fork.

6 Brush both sides of the bread with oil. Place under a preheated broiler at the highest setting. Cook for 3 minutes, turn the bread over and cook for a further 3 minutes. It should have dark brown spots all over.

7 Spread a teaspoonful of the apple purée all over the bread, then sprinkle over a quarter of the golden raisins, the slivered almonds, the cilantro leaves, and the coconut. Repeat with the remaining 3 ovals of dough.

Step *4*

Step *5*

Step *7*

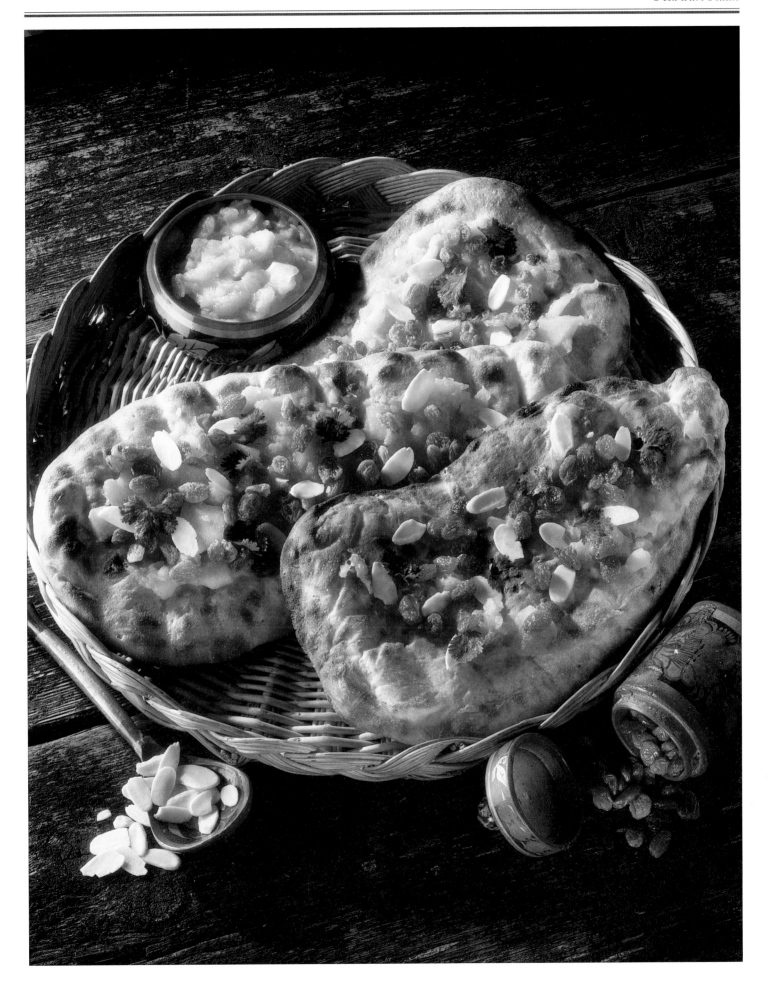

Spicy Oven Bread

***This Western-style bread has been adapted with Indian ingredients.
It is quite a rich mix and very tasty.***

SERVES 4

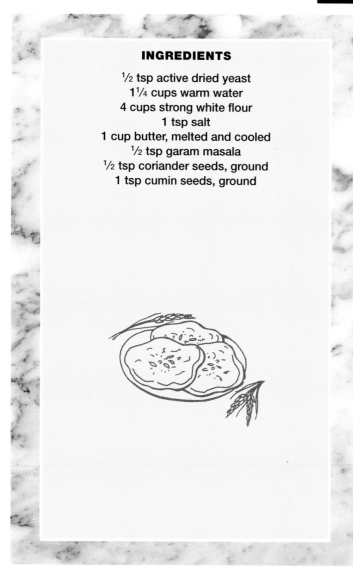

INGREDIENTS

½ tsp active dried yeast
1¼ cups warm water
4 cups strong white flour
1 tsp salt
1 cup butter, melted and cooled
½ tsp garam masala
½ tsp coriander seeds, ground
1 tsp cumin seeds, ground

1 Mix the yeast with a little of the warm water until it starts to foam and is completely dissolved.

2 Put the flour and salt into a large bowl, make a well in the center, and add the yeast mixture and ½ cup of the melted butter. Blend the yeast and butter together before drawing in the flour and kneading lightly. Gradually add enough water to form a firm dough – you may not need it all.

3 Turn the dough out and knead until smooth and elastic, about 10 minutes. Put the dough into an oiled bowl, turning to coat. Cover and leave in a warm place to rise until doubled, about 30 minutes. Alternatively, leave in the refrigerator overnight.

4 Punch down the dough and divide into 8 balls. Roll each ball out to about a 6 in. round. Put onto a floured cookie sheet. Sprinkle with flour and leave for 20 minutes.

5 Mix the spices with the remaining melted butter.

6 Brush each bread with the spice and butter mixture and cover with foil. Place on the middle shelf of a preheated oven at 425°F for 5 minutes. Remove the foil, brush with the butter once again, and cook for a further 5 minutes.

7 Remove from the oven and wrap in a clean dishcloth until ready to eat.

Step *2*

Step *4*

Step *6*

Parathas

*These triangular-shaped breads are so easy to make and are the perfect addition
to most Indian meals. Serve hot, spread with a little butter, if wished.*

MAKES 6

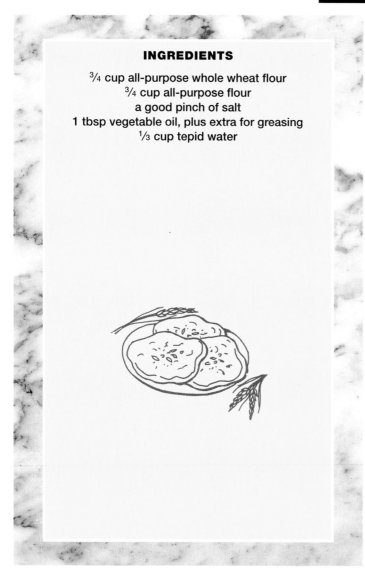

INGREDIENTS

¾ cup all-purpose whole wheat flour
¾ cup all-purpose flour
a good pinch of salt
1 tbsp vegetable oil, plus extra for greasing
⅓ cup tepid water

1 Place the flours and the salt in a bowl. Drizzle 1 tablespoon of oil over the flour, add the tepid water, and mix to form a soft dough, adding a little more water, if necessary. Knead on a lightly floured surface until smooth, then cover, and leave for 30 minutes.

2 Knead the dough on a floured surface and divide into 6 equal pieces. Shape each one into a ball. Roll out on a floured surface to a 6 in. round and brush very lightly with oil.

3 Fold in half, and then in half again to form a triangle. Roll out to form a 7 in. triangle (when measured from point to center top), dusting with extra flour as necessary.

4 Brush a large skillet with a little oil and heat until hot, then add one or two parathas, and cook for about 1–1½ minutes. Brush the surfaces very lightly with oil, then turn, and cook the other sides for 1½ minutes until cooked through.

5 Place the cooked parathas on a plate and cover with foil or place between a clean dishcloth to keep warm, while you cook the remainder in the same way, greasing the skillet between cooking each batch.

Step *2*

Step *3*

Step *4*

Stuffed Parathas

To make parathas successfully, be sure to knead the dough until it is quite smooth and to roll it out as thinly as you can.

SERVES 4–8

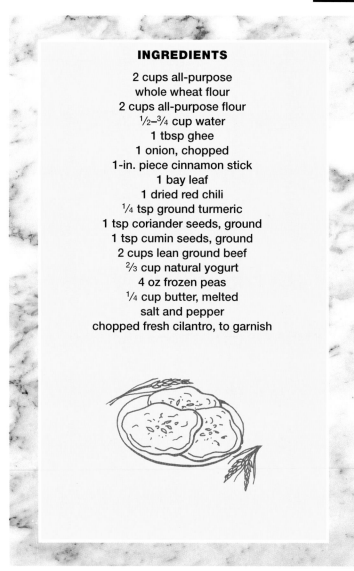

INGREDIENTS

2 cups all-purpose
whole wheat flour
2 cups all-purpose flour
½–¾ cup water
1 tbsp ghee
1 onion, chopped
1-in. piece cinnamon stick
1 bay leaf
1 dried red chili
¼ tsp ground turmeric
1 tsp coriander seeds, ground
1 tsp cumin seeds, ground
2 cups lean ground beef
⅔ cup natural yogurt
4 oz frozen peas
¼ cup butter, melted
salt and pepper
chopped fresh cilantro, to garnish

1 Sift the two flours and a pinch of salt together into a bowl and make a well in the center.

2 Gradually add enough water to make a soft dough, and knead until smooth and no longer sticky. Set aside.

3 Heat the ghee in a large skillet and fry the onion until golden brown. Add the cinnamon, bay leaf, chili, turmeric, coriander, cumin, and ground beef, and stir for 1 minute. Add the yogurt and cook over a high heat until the beef is dry. Add the peas, season to taste, then simmer for 8–10 minutes.

4 To make the parathas, divide the dough into 6 or 8 pieces. Roll each piece into a ball, then roll out to a 10 in. round.

5 Brush the upper side with melted butter. Fold in half, and spoon 1 tablespoon of the stuffing into the center of each folded piece. Fold each half in half again so that you are left with cone shapes.

6 Gently heat a large skillet and place a paratha in it. Brush each side lightly with a little melted butter and cook over a medium heat for 3–4 minutes. Do not let the pan get too hot. Turn over and cook the other side for 3–4 minutes. Keep warm and repeat with the remaining parathas. Serve immediately.

Step *1*

Step *4*

Step *5*

Shrimp Pooris

Tiger shrimp are especially good cooked this way, although the less expensive, smaller peeled shrimp may be used instead.

SERVES 6

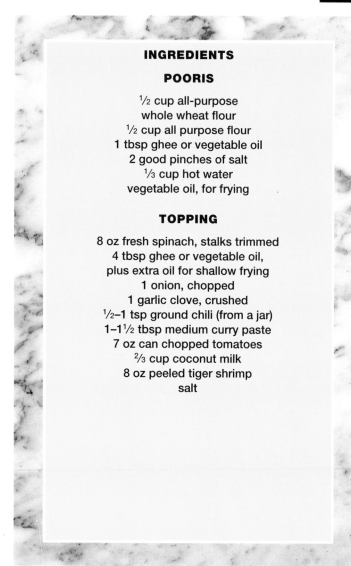

INGREDIENTS

POORIS

½ cup all-purpose
whole wheat flour
½ cup all purpose flour
1 tbsp ghee or vegetable oil
2 good pinches of salt
⅓ cup hot water
vegetable oil, for frying

TOPPING

8 oz fresh spinach, stalks trimmed
4 tbsp ghee or vegetable oil,
plus extra oil for shallow frying
1 onion, chopped
1 garlic clove, crushed
½–1 tsp ground chili (from a jar)
1–1½ tbsp medium curry paste
7 oz can chopped tomatoes
⅔ cup coconut milk
8 oz peeled tiger shrimp
salt

1 To make the pooris, put the flours in a bowl and make a well in the center. Add the ghee or oil, salt, and hot water and mix to form a dough. Leave to stand for 1 hour.

2 Meanwhile, prepare the topping. Cut the spinach crosswise into wide strips – do this by making bundles of leaves and slicing with a sharp knife.

3 Heat the ghee or oil in a skillet, add the onion, garlic, chili, and spinach, and cook gently for 4 minutes, shaking the skillet and stirring frequently. Add the curry paste, tomatoes, and coconut milk and simmer for 10 minutes, stirring occasionally. Remove from the heat, stir in the shrimp, and season with salt to taste.

4 Knead the dough well on a floured surface, divide into 6 pieces, and shape into 6 balls. Roll out each one to a 5 in. round. Heat about 1 in. oil in a deep skillet until smoking hot. Take one poori at a time, lower into the hot oil, and cook for 10–15 seconds on each side until puffed up and golden. Remove the poori with a slotted spoon, drain on absorbent paper towels, and keep warm while cooking the remainder in the same way.

5 Reheat the shrimp mixture, stirring until piping hot. Arrange a poori on each serving plate and spoon the shrimp and spinach mixture onto each one. Serve immediately.

Step *1*

Step *4*

Step *5*

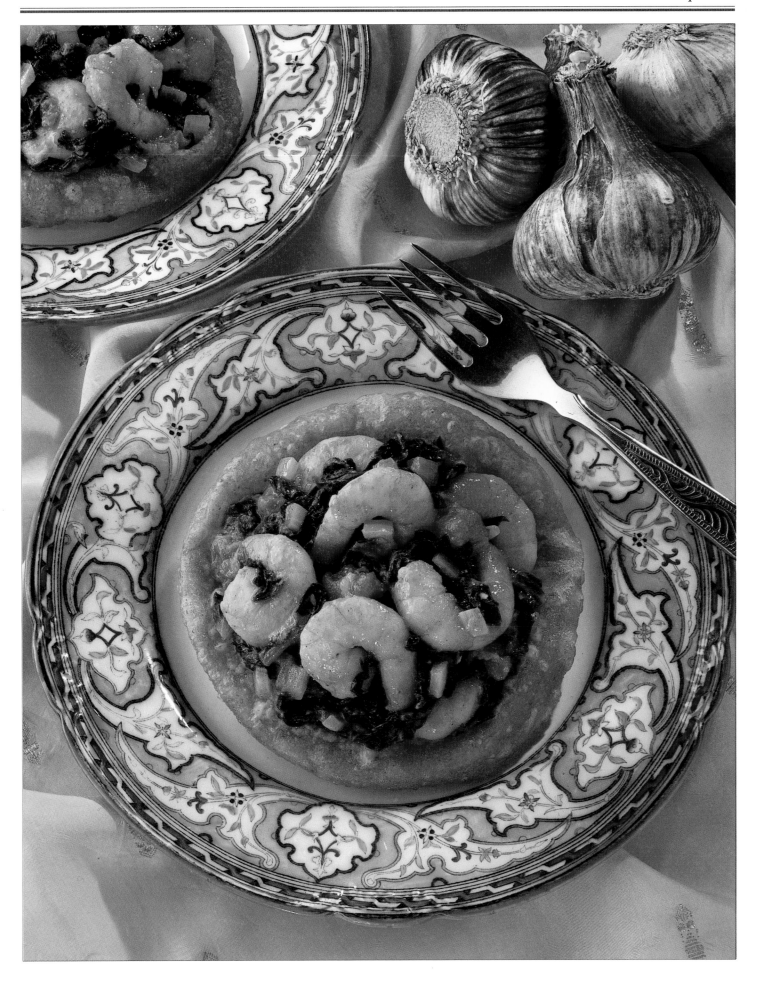

Mixed Bell Pepper Pooris

Whole wheat pooris are easy to make and so good to eat served with a topping of spicy mixed bell peppers and yogurt.

SERVES 6

INGREDIENTS

POORIS

1 cup all-purpose
whole wheat flour
1 tbsp vegetable ghee or oil
2 good pinches of salt
1/3 cup hot water
vegetable oil, for shallow frying
natural yogurt, to serve
sprigs of cilantro, to garnish

TOPPING

4 tbsp vegetable ghee or oil
1 large onion, quartered and thinly sliced
1/2 red bell pepper,
deseeded and thinly sliced
1/2 green bell pepper,
deseeded and thinly sliced
1/4 eggplant, cut lengthwise
into 6 wedges and sliced thinly
1 garlic clove, crushed
1-in. piece ginger root, chopped finely
1/2–1 tsp ground chili (from a jar)
2 tsp mild or medium curry paste
7 oz can chopped tomatoes
salt

1 To make the pooris, put the flour in a bowl with the ghee or oil and salt. Add hot water and mix to form a fairly soft dough. Knead gently, cover with a damp cloth, and leave for 30 minutes.

2 Meanwhile, prepare the topping. Heat the ghee or oil in a large saucepan, add the onion, bell peppers, eggplant, garlic, ginger, chili, and curry paste, and fry gently for 5 minutes. Stir in the tomatoes and salt to taste. Simmer gently, uncovered, for 5 minutes, stirring occasionally until the sauce thickens. Remove from the heat.

3 Knead the dough on a floured surface. Divide into 6. Roll each piece to a round about 6 inches in diameter. Cover each one as you finish rolling, to prevent it from drying out.

4 Heat about 1/2 in. oil in a large skillet. Add the pooris, one at a time, and fry for about 15 seconds on each side until puffed and golden, turning frequently. Drain on paper towels and keep warm while cooking the remainder in the same way.

5 Reheat the vegetable mixture. Place a poori on each serving plate and top with the vegetable mixture. Add a spoonful of yogurt to each one and garnish with sprigs of cilantro. Serve hot.

Step *1*

Step *3*

Step *5*

Spinach Poori

These little nibbles are very satisfying to make. Don't be slow in serving them and they will still be little puffballs when you get to the table.

SERVES 6

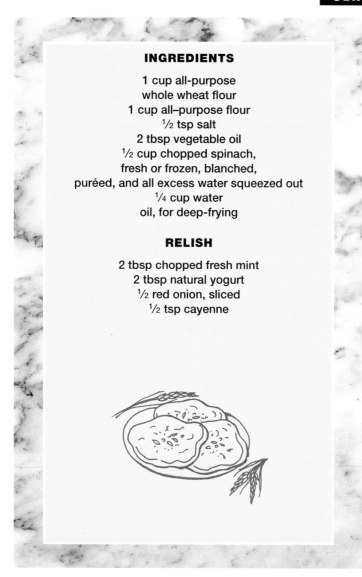

INGREDIENTS

1 cup all-purpose
whole wheat flour
1 cup all–purpose flour
½ tsp salt
2 tbsp vegetable oil
½ cup chopped spinach,
fresh or frozen, blanched,
puréed, and all excess water squeezed out
¼ cup water
oil, for deep-frying

RELISH

2 tbsp chopped fresh mint
2 tbsp natural yogurt
½ red onion, sliced
½ tsp cayenne

1 Sift the flours and salt together into a bowl. Drizzle over the oil and rub in until the mixture resembles fine breadcrumbs.

2 Add the spinach and enough water to make a stiff dough. Knead for 10 minutes until smooth.

3 Form the dough into a ball. Put into an oiled bowl and turn to coat. Cover with plastic wrap and set aside for 30 minutes.

4 Meanwhile make the relish. Combine the mint, yogurt, and onion, transfer to a serving bowl and sift the cayenne over the top.

5 Knead the dough again and divide into 12 small balls. Remove 1 ball and keep the rest covered. Roll this ball out into a 5 in. round.

6 Put the oil into a wok or wide skillet to 1 in. depth. Heat it until a haze appears. It must be very hot.

7 Have ready a plate lined with paper towels. Put 1 poori on the surface of the oil – if it sinks, it should rise up immediately and sizzle; if it doesn't, the oil isn't hot enough. Keep the poori submerged in the oil, using the back of a spatula or a perforated spoon. The poori will puff up immediately. Turn it over and cook the other side for 5–10 seconds.

8 As soon as the poori is cooked, remove and drain. Repeat with the remaining balls of dough.

Step *2*

Step *5*

Step *7*

CHUTNEYS, PICKLES, & RELISHES

In the Indian subcontinent the heat is often so intense and enveloping that it is essential for every cook to have in his or her repertoire a range of pickle and chutney recipes containing ingredients that can be preserved regardless of the heat. Salt, oil, vinegar, and citric acid can all be used as a means of preserving, depending on the desired effect.

These preserves have claimed their place in the grand scheme of Indian gastronomy – no table would be complete without a selection of pickles presented on a tray for you to dip into. Who can imagine eating a dry, spicy, tender dish without a yogurt accompaniment? Or crisp poppadoms without the mango chutney? Not only do Indian pickles and preserves accompany meat and fish, but because vegetarianism is such a way of life in India, they are devised to complement the meat-free meals too.

Chili Chutney

Surprisingly enough an Indian meal isn't always hot enough for everybody. This chutney will give a bite to the meal, as well as a zingy lime freshener to the palate.

SERVES 6

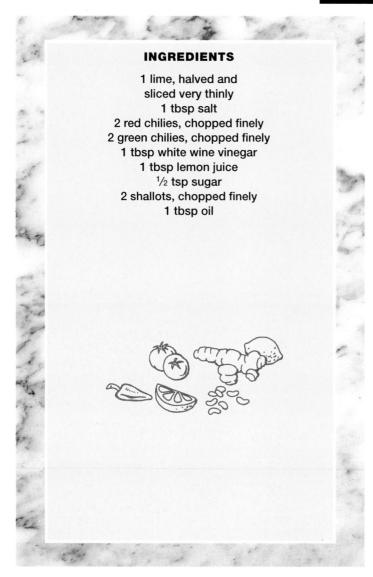

INGREDIENTS

1 lime, halved and
sliced very thinly
1 tbsp salt
2 red chilies, chopped finely
2 green chilies, chopped finely
1 tbsp white wine vinegar
1 tbsp lemon juice
½ tsp sugar
2 shallots, chopped finely
1 tbsp oil

1 Combine the lime slices with the salt. Leave to stand for 30 minutes.

2 Mix the chilies with the vinegar. Stir for a few seconds, then drain.

3 Mix together the chilies, lemon juice, sugar, chopped shallots, and oil.

4 Add the salted limes to the chili mixture, mixing thoroughly.

5 Transfer the chutney to a non-staining serving dish. Serve as an accompaniment to any mild or rich curry.

Step *1*

Step *3*

Step *4*

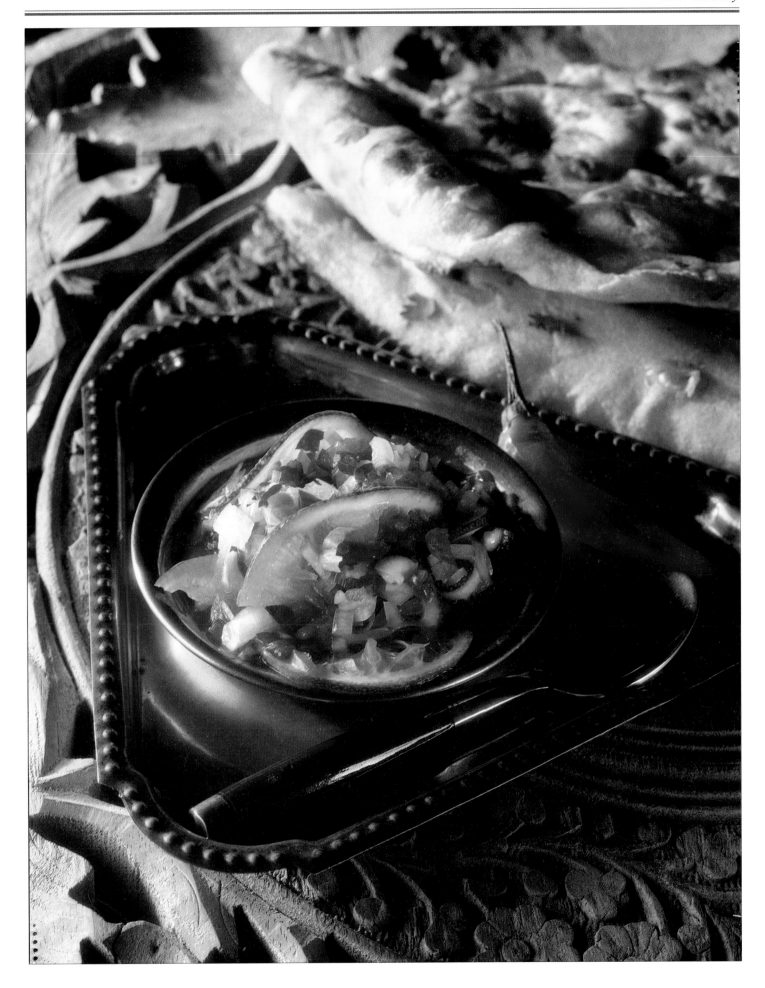

Walnut Chutney & Garlic Chutney

This delicious chutney complements the Butterfly Shrimp on page 20. The Garlic Chutney has a hotter flavor.

SERVES 4-6

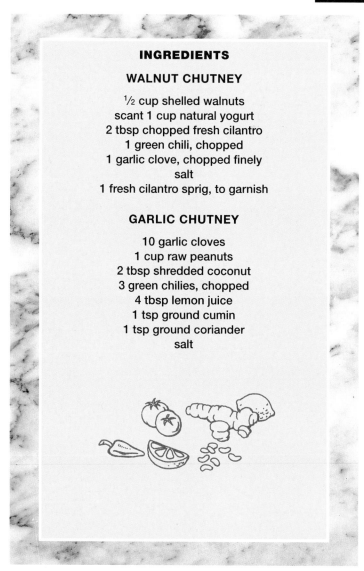

INGREDIENTS

WALNUT CHUTNEY

½ cup shelled walnuts
scant 1 cup natural yogurt
2 tbsp chopped fresh cilantro
1 green chili, chopped
1 garlic clove, chopped finely
salt
1 fresh cilantro sprig, to garnish

GARLIC CHUTNEY

10 garlic cloves
1 cup raw peanuts
2 tbsp shredded coconut
3 green chilies, chopped
4 tbsp lemon juice
1 tsp ground cumin
1 tsp ground coriander
salt

1 Grind in a spice grinder or chop finely by hand ¼ cup of the walnuts. Chop the remaining walnuts roughly by hand.

2 Combine the chopped and ground walnuts, mixing thoroughly.

3 Stir in the yogurt, cilantro, chili, and garlic. Season to taste. You will find the chutney thickens a lot at this stage. Transfer to a serving dish and garnish with cilantro. This will keep for 1–2 days in the refrigerator.

4 To make the Garlic Chutney, put all the ingredients into a food processor and grind with enough water to make a paste. Alternatively, use a pestle and mortar.

5 Leave to stand for an hour before serving. This will keep for 1–2 days in the refrigerator.

Step *1*

Step *2*

Step *3*

Lime Pickle

This is the hottest and most thirst-making of the Indian pickles. Ginger pickle is the sweetest, but lime pickle is the one that will have you going back for more.

SERVES 8

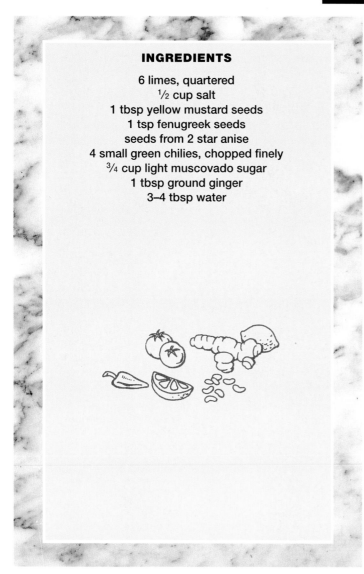

INGREDIENTS

6 limes, quartered
½ cup salt
1 tbsp yellow mustard seeds
1 tsp fenugreek seeds
seeds from 2 star anise
4 small green chilies, chopped finely
¾ cup light muscovado sugar
1 tbsp ground ginger
3–4 tbsp water

1 Put the limes into a large bowl and sprinkle over the salt. Leave for 24 hours.

2 Next day, put the mustard seeds, fenugreek, star anise seeds, and chilies into a saucepan and cover. Place over a high heat and roast the spices, shaking the pan constantly until the mustard seeds start to pop. Remove from the heat.

3 Strain the liquid from the limes into a small pan. Add the sugar, ginger, and water. Boil for 2 minutes or until the sugar has dissolved.

4 Combine the limes and spices and put into 2 clean, dry preserving jars. Pour over the sugar solution, making sure that it covers the limes. If it doesn't, cram the limes further down into the jar, or remove one or two quarters.

5 Cover the jars loosely, and when quite cool, screw on the lids tightly. Label each jar, adding the date on which the pickle was made. Keep in a cool place for 4 weeks before using.

Step *2*

Step *3*

Step *4*

Tomato, Onion, & Cucumber Kachumber

This is a relish that is served at all Indian tables as a palate refresher or an appetizer. Two variations on the main recipe are included here.

SERVES 6

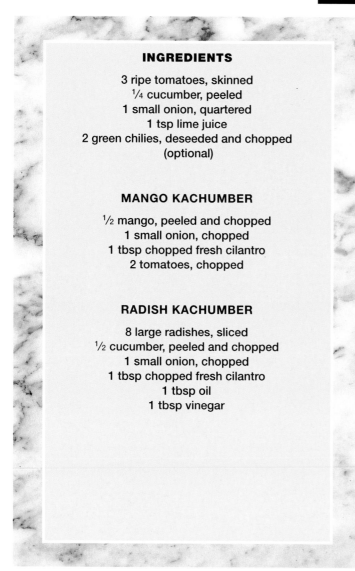

INGREDIENTS

3 ripe tomatoes, skinned
¼ cucumber, peeled
1 small onion, quartered
1 tsp lime juice
2 green chilies, deseeded and chopped
(optional)

MANGO KACHUMBER

½ mango, peeled and chopped
1 small onion, chopped
1 tbsp chopped fresh cilantro
2 tomatoes, chopped

RADISH KACHUMBER

8 large radishes, sliced
½ cucumber, peeled and chopped
1 small onion, chopped
1 tbsp chopped fresh cilantro
1 tbsp oil
1 tbsp vinegar

1 Cut the tomatoes into quarters, then cut each quarter in half lengthwise. The seeds can be removed at this stage, if you prefer.

2 Cut the cucumber lengthwise into quarters. Remove the seeds, and cut the flesh into cubes.

3 Cut each onion quarter into slices.

4 Combine all the ingredients in a bowl and sprinkle with lime juice. Add the chilies, if using, and serve.

MANGO KACHUMBER

1 Combine all the ingredients in a bowl, and serve.

RADISH KACHUMBER

1 Combine all the ingredients in a bowl, and serve.

Step *1*

Step *2*

Step *3*

Cucumber Raita

In any Indian restaurant, the first thing to be brought to the table should be a kachumber salad and a raita, which you eat with a few poppadoms.

SERVES 4

INGREDIENTS

2 tsp fresh mint
½ cucumber
1 cup natural yogurt
salt and pepper
freshly grated nutmeg, to garnish

GRAPEFRUIT RAITA

1 tsp sugar
1 tsp finely grated grapefruit rind
½ grapefruit, segmented
1 cup natural yogurt
salt and pepper

MELON RAITA

¼ honeydew or firm melon, peeled, and cut into
½ in. cubes
¼ medium pineapple, peeled and cut into
½ in. cubes
1 tsp cayenne
1 tsp ground coriander seeds
1 cup natural yogurt
salt and pepper

DATE RAITA

6 dates, chopped
1 tbsp raisins
1 crisp green apple, chopped
1 cup natural yogurt
salt and pepper

1 Chop the mint finely using a sharp knife.

2 Peel the cucumber, remove the seeds, and cut the flesh into matchsticks.

3 Combine the cucumber with the yogurt and mint. Season with salt and pepper to taste.

4 Turn the mixture into a serving dish and sprinkle with nutmeg before serving.

GRAPEFRUIT RAITA

1 Combine all the ingredients and serve immediately. This version should be eaten on the day you make it, as it does not keep well.

MELON RAITA

1 Combine the melon and pineapple cubes, cayenne, ground coriander seeds, and salt and pepper in a bowl. Stir in the yogurt and serve. This will keep for 1–2 days in the refrigerator.

DATE RAITA

1 Combine all these ingredients in a bowl and serve. This will keep for 1–2 days in the refrigerator.

Step *1*

Step *2*

Step *3*

DESSERTS

Indian-style meals are traditionally rounded off with something very sweet or with a large selection of carefully-prepared plain fresh fruit, such as mangoes, guavas, melon, and pears. These are best served well chilled, especially in the summer months, and can make a welcome change or contrast to a spicy, warm, aromatic main course feast.

For a stunning finale to an Indian meal, dice, slice, or cut the fruit into colorful wedges, then arrange them on a huge platter with sprigs of mint.

The simplest, and often most appreciated dessert is a cooling kulfi or ice-cream. Many are served plain, but others are flavored with mango and coconut. They are delicious sprinkled with chopped shelled pistachios or almonds.

Mango Ice-Cream

This delicious ice-cream with its refreshing tang of mango and lime makes the perfect ending to a hot and spicy meal.

SERVES 4-6

INGREDIENTS

²⁄₃ cup light cream
2 egg yolks
¹⁄₂ tsp cornstarch
1 tsp water
2 × 14 oz cans mango slices in syrup,
drained
1 tbsp lime or lemon juice
²⁄₃ cup heavy cream
sprigs of mint, to decorate

1 Heat the light cream in a saucepan until hot (but do not allow it to boil). Place the egg yolks in a bowl with the cornstarch and water and mix together until smooth. Pour the hot cream onto the egg yolk mixture, stirring all the time.

2 Return the mixture to the pan and place over a very low heat, beating or stirring all the time until the mixture thickens and coats the back of a wooden spoon. (Do not try to hurry this process or the mixture will overcook and spoil.) Pour into a bowl.

3 Purée the drained mango slices in a blender or food processor until smooth, or chop finely, mash with a fork, and push through a strainer. Mix with the custard and stir in the lime juice. Whip the heavy cream until soft peaks form. Fold into the mango mixture until thoroughly combined.

4 Transfer the mixture to a loaf pan or shallow freezerproof container. Cover and freeze for 2–3 hours or until half-frozen and still mushy in the center. Turn the mixture into a bowl and mash well with a fork until smooth. Return to the container, cover, and freeze again until firm.

5 Transfer the container of ice-cream to the main compartment of the refrigerator for about 30 minutes before serving to allow it to soften slightly. Scoop or spoon the ice-cream into serving dishes and decorate with sprigs of mint.

Step *1*

Step *2*

Step *4*

Bananas with Spiced Yogurt & Almonds

*This simple but delicious dessert is at its nicest when made with
thick and creamy yogurt.*

SERVES 4–6

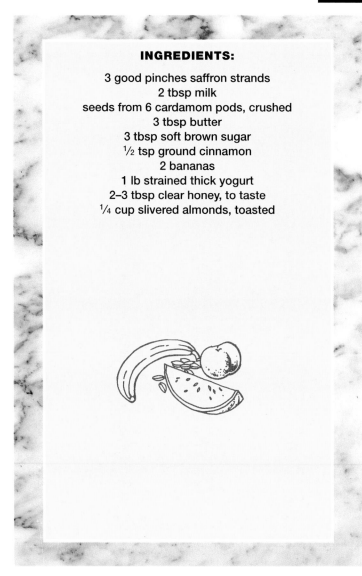

INGREDIENTS:

3 good pinches saffron strands
2 tbsp milk
seeds from 6 cardamom pods, crushed
3 tbsp butter
3 tbsp soft brown sugar
½ tsp ground cinnamon
2 bananas
1 lb strained thick yogurt
2–3 tbsp clear honey, to taste
¼ cup slivered almonds, toasted

1 Place the saffron strands on a small piece of foil and toast very lightly. Crush the saffron strands finely and place in a small bowl.

2 Add the milk and crushed cardamom seeds, stir well, and leave to cool.

3 Meanwhile, melt the butter in a skillet, add the sugar and cinnamon, and stir well. Peel and slice the bananas and fry gently for about 1 minute, turning halfway through cooking. Remove from the skillet and place the fried banana slices in sundae glasses.

4 Mix the yogurt with the cold spiced milk and the honey. Spoon the mixture on top of the bananas and liberally sprinkle the surface of each serving with toasted slivered almonds. Chill before serving, if preferred.

Step *1*

Step *2*

Step *4*

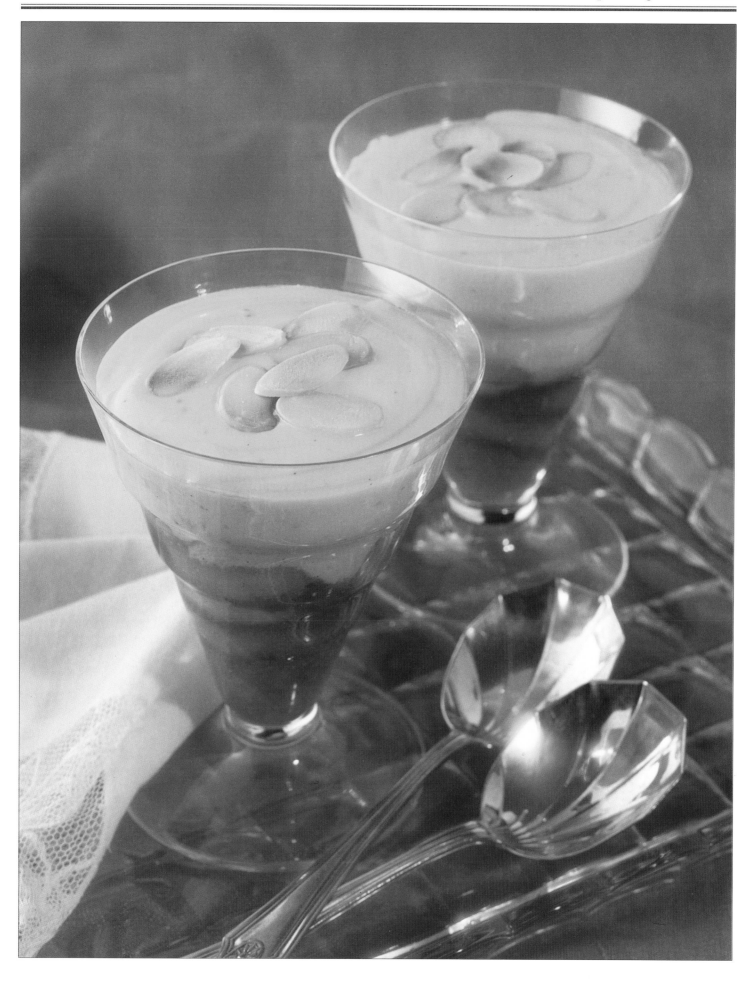

Coconut Ice-Cream

This delicious ice-cream will make the perfect ending to any Indian meal.
For a smooth-textured dessert leave out the coconut.

SERVES 6

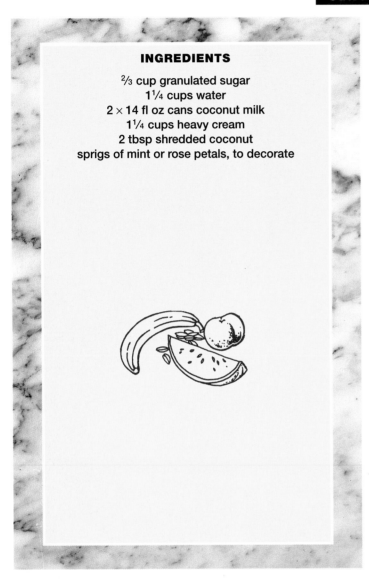

INGREDIENTS

⅔ cup granulated sugar
1¼ cups water
2 × 14 fl oz cans coconut milk
1¼ cups heavy cream
2 tbsp shredded coconut
sprigs of mint or rose petals, to decorate

1 Place the sugar and water in a saucepan and heat gently, stirring occasionally, until the sugar dissolves. Boil gently for 10 minutes without stirring, then remove from the heat, and allow to cool slightly.

2 Mix the cooled syrup with the coconut milk and pour into a shallow freezer container. Cover and freeze for about 3 hours or until semi-frozen around the edges and mushy in the center.

3 Transfer the mixture to a bowl and cut up with a knife, then place (half the quantity at a time) in a food processor, and process until smooth, or beat thoroughly by hand.

4 Turn the mixture into a bowl. Whip the cream until soft peaks form and fold into the ice-cream, then stir in the shredded coconut. Return the mixture to the container and freeze again until solid.

5 Before serving, put the container in the refrigerator and leave for 30 minutes (or leave at room temperature for 15 minutes) to soften. Scoop or spoon the ice-cream into serving dishes and decorate with sprigs of mint or rose petals.

Step *2*

Step *3*

Step *4*

Mango & Yogurt Cream

*This wonderfully refreshing dessert is designed to help refresh
the palate after a hot and spicy meal.*

SERVES 6

INGREDIENTS

2 large ripe mangoes
2 tbsp lime juice
2 tbsp superfine sugar
⅔ cup heavy cream
⅔ cup strained thick yogurt
seeds from 4 cardamom pods, crushed,
lime twists or zest, to decorate

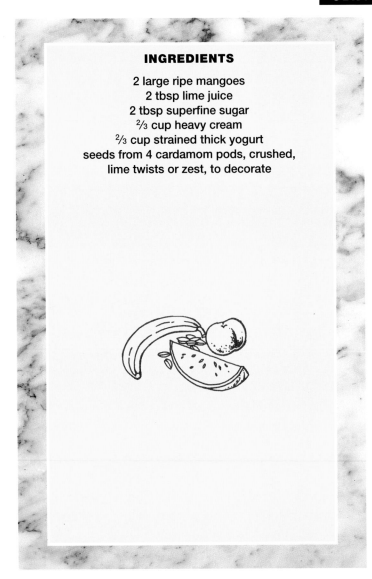

1 To prepare each mango, cut along either side of the large central pit, to give two halves of mango. Cut off any flesh attached to the pit, and remove the peel.

2 Place the flesh in a blender or food processor with the lime juice and sugar and process until the mixture forms a smooth purée, or chop the flesh, mash with a fork, and push through a strainer. Turn the mixture into a bowl.

3 Whip the cream in a bowl until stiff, then fold in the yogurt and the crushed cardamom seeds.

4 Reserve 4 tablespoons of the mango purée for decoration, and mix the remaining mango purée into the cream and yogurt mixture.

5 Spoon the mixture into sundae glasses. Drizzle a little of the reserved mango sauce over each dessert and serve chilled, decorated with lime twists.

Step *1*

Step *3*

Step *4*

Indian Ice-Cream (Kulfi)

*To make traditional Kulfi is quite a time-consuming process,
so why not try this deliciously easy version instead?*

SERVES 6–8

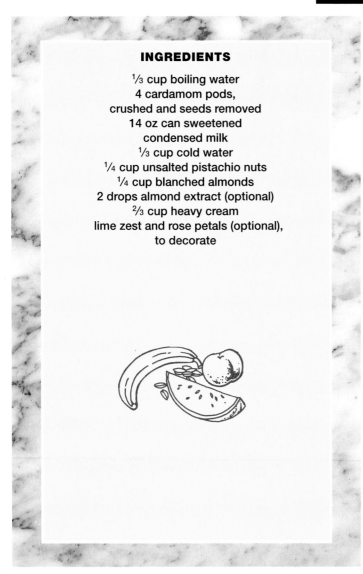

INGREDIENTS

⅓ cup boiling water
4 cardamom pods,
crushed and seeds removed
14 oz can sweetened
condensed milk
⅓ cup cold water
¼ cup unsalted pistachio nuts
¼ cup blanched almonds
2 drops almond extract (optional)
⅔ cup heavy cream
lime zest and rose petals (optional),
to decorate

1 Pour the boiling water into a bowl, stir in the cardamom seeds, and leave for 15 minutes to infuse.

2 Meanwhile, put the condensed milk into a blender or food processor together with the cold water, pistachio nuts, almonds, and almond extract, if using. Process the mixture for about 30 seconds until very finely mixed.

3 Add the cooled and strained cardamom water and pour into a bowl. Whip the cream until soft peaks form. Whip into the mixture. Pour into a shallow metal or plastic container and freeze for about 3 hours or until semi-frozen around the edges and mushy in the center.

4 Transfer the mixture to a bowl and mash well with a fork (to break up the ice crystals). Divide the mixture evenly between 6–8 small molds and freeze for at least 4 hours or overnight until firm.

5 To serve, dip the base of each mold quickly into hot water and run a knife around the top edge. Turn out onto serving plates and decorate with lime zest and rose petals, if using.

Step *1*

Step *3*

Step *4*

Saffron-Spiced Rice Pudding

*This rich and comforting pudding is cooked in milk delicately flavored
with saffron and cinnamon.*

SERVES 4–5

INGREDIENTS

2½ cups milk
several pinches of saffron strands,
finely crushed
¼ cup pudding rice
1 cinnamon stick or piece of cassia bark
1½ oz sugar
¼ cup seedless raisins or golden raisins
¼ cup no-need-to-soak dried apricots, chopped
1 egg, beaten
⅓ cup light cream
1 tbsp butter, diced
2 tbsp slivered almonds
freshly grated nutmeg, for sprinkling
cream (optional), to serve

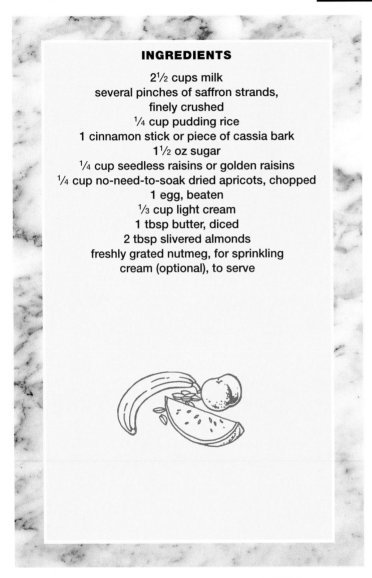

1 Place the milk and crushed saffron in a non-stick saucepan and bring to a boil. Stir in the rice and cinnamon stick, reduce the heat, and simmer very gently, uncovered, for 25 minutes, stirring frequently until the rice is tender.

2 Remove the pan from the heat and discard the cinnamon stick. Stir in the sugar, raisins, and apricots, then beat in the egg, cream, and diced butter.

3 Transfer the mixture to a greased ovenproof pie or flan dish, sprinkle with the almonds and freshly grated nutmeg, to taste. Place in a preheated oven, 325°F, for 25–30 minutes until the mixture is set and lightly golden. Serve hot with extra cream, if wished.

Step *1*

Step *2*

Step *3*

Aromatic Fruit Salad

*The fruits in this dessert are arranged attractively on serving plates
with the spicy syrup spooned over.*

SERVES 6

INGREDIENTS

3 tbsp sugar
¾ cup water
1 cinnamon stick or large piece of cassia bark
4 cardamom pods, crushed
1 clove
juice of 1 orange
2 tbsp lime juice
½ honeydew melon
good-sized wedge of watermelon
2 ripe guavas
3 ripe nectarines
about 18 strawberries
a little toasted, shredded coconut for sprinkling
sprigs of mint or rose petals, to decorate
strained thick yogurt, to serve

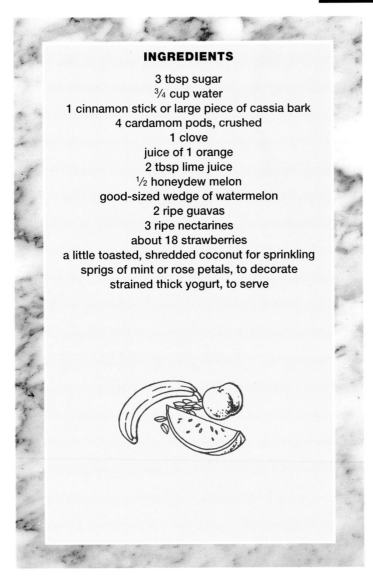

1 First prepare the syrup. Put the sugar, water, cinnamon, cardamom pods, and clove into a pan and bring to a boil, stirring to dissolve the sugar.

2 Simmer for 2 minutes, then remove from the heat. Add the orange and lime juices, then leave to cool and infuse while you prepare the fruits.

3 Peel and remove the seeds from the melons and cut the flesh into neat slices. Cut the guavas in half, scoop out the seeds, then peel, and slice the flesh neatly. Cut the nectarines into slices, and hull and slice the strawberries.

4 Arrange the slices of fruit attractively on 6 serving plates. Strain the cooled syrup and spoon over the sliced fruits. Sprinkle with a little toasted coconut. Decorate each serving with sprigs of mint or rose petals and serve with yogurt, if wished.

Step *1*

Step *2*

Step *3*

Sweet Carrot Halva

*This nutritious dessert, made from grated carrots simmered in milk,
is flavored with spices, nuts, and raisins.*

SERVES 6

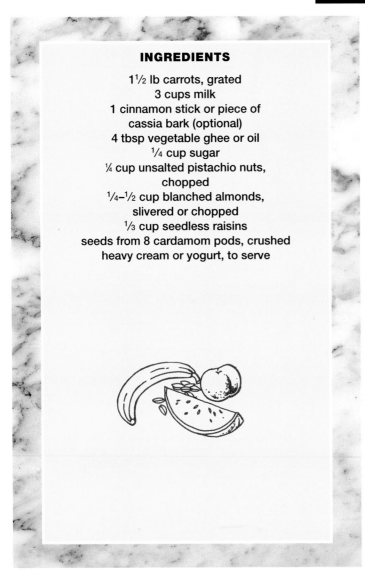

INGREDIENTS

1½ lb carrots, grated
3 cups milk
1 cinnamon stick or piece of
cassia bark (optional)
4 tbsp vegetable ghee or oil
¼ cup sugar
¼ cup unsalted pistachio nuts,
chopped
¼–½ cup blanched almonds,
slivered or chopped
⅓ cup seedless raisins
seeds from 8 cardamom pods, crushed
heavy cream or yogurt, to serve

1 Put the grated carrots, milk, and cinnamon or cassia, if using, into a large, heavy-based saucepan and bring to a boil. Reduce the heat to a simmer and cook, uncovered, for 35–40 minutes, or until thickened (with no milk remaining). Stir the mixture frequently during cooking to prevent its sticking. Discard the cinnamon.

2 Heat the ghee or oil in a non-stick skillet, add the carrot mixture, and stir-fry over a medium heat for about 5 minutes or until the carrots take on a glossy sheen.

3 Add the sugar, pistachios, almonds, raisins, and crushed cardamom seeds, mix well, and continue frying for a further 3–4 minutes, stirring frequently. Serve warm or cold with cream or yogurt.

Step *1*

Step *2*

Step *3*

INDEX